summer 2020

The Untold Story of Donald J. Trump,
Black Lives Matter, and Diversity

Ramsey Jeremie

© 2020 Ramsey Jeremie

All rights reserved.

No part of this publication in print or in electronic format may be reproduced, stored in a retrieval system, or transmitted in any form or by any means, electronic, mechanical, photocopying, recording, or otherwise without the prior written permission of the publisher.

The scanning, uploading, and distribution of this book without permission is a theft of the author's intellectual property. If you would like permission to use material from the book (other than for review purposes), please contact info@bublish.com. Thank you for your support of the author's rights.

Distribution by Bublish, Inc.

Paperback ISBN: 978-1-64704-268-4
eBook ISBN: 978-1-64704-269-1

Introduction

The Summer of 2020 was a time of confusion, misinformation, anxiety, skepticism, uncertainty, tragedy, and, unfortunately, death. It was an unprecedented summer in an unprecedented year that felt at times almost stranger than fiction. While the main characters of this book, Donald Trump and Black Lives Matter, have certainly had a contentious relationship during Trump's presidency, I would not classify them as typical political rivals as, let's say, Republicans and Democrats. In my opinion, Donald Trump and Black Lives Matter have a more philosophical—possibly even fundamental—human rivalry: the "establishment" vs the "revolution," the "oppressor" versus the "oppressed," "authority" vs "change." This story does not attempt to morally evaluate the motivations or intentions of Donald Trump and Black Lives Matter but serves more to critically understand how these two "characters" represent America's struggle to establish a national identity. "Diversity's" session attempts to place this "rivalry" in a more global and historic context, so that we can better understand and potentially reconcile with the dynamics and nature of human conflict. While this story is presented to you as a book, I've written it with a screenplay aesthetic, so that you can read through it like you are watching a movie or binging a television series. My hope is that you feel as though history is unfolding in front of you, because that is certainly what living through the summer of 2020 felt like. This book was inspired by and written during this time, but, nevertheless, it is fictional and should ultimately be read that way. As the reader, I only ask that if you find yourself questioning the authenticity of these accounts, to stop and consider why that might be.

Dedication

This book is dedicated to anybody with whom I have waxed poetically about life. Your conversation has indirectly or directly influenced this book.

To Gavriel, this is as close to a doctorate as I'll ever get. So proud of you, man!
To Meagan, for being such a great editor in the manuscript of my life.
To Justin, for being the best road trip buddy on the highway of life.
To Brandon, for being the best hype man.
To Ayoosh, for being my poetry partner in crime.

Special thanks to my mom, dad, and sister, whose love, support, and Haitian criticism has carried me to heights I would have never striven to reach!

And the most special of thanks goes to my wife, Bailey, whose unyielding faith in me, support, and sacrifice made this book possible.

■ ■ ■

Rain spatters on windowsills and a door abruptly opens and closes.
"Wheewww, I guess it's fall! that rain is soo cold…"
Keys clang on the countertop, an umbrella shakes and contracts.
"Honey!!?? Kids? Anybody home?"
Woof! Woof!
"Hey, Sawyer! How are you! Who's a good dog, who's a good dog… did someone feed you? Huh? You hungry? Alright, let me get a treat for you…"
A cabinet door creaks open.
"Might as well get something for myself, too…it's going to be a long night. Let's see here…Jade Mint, Lavender…Ahh, Vanilla Roibos, perfect!"
The cabinet door shuts, the stove is turned on, a kettle whistles, and a dining room chair creaks as it is pulled out from table.
"Alright, let's see here…feels good to be off my feet…hmmm…who should we start off with?? Oops, water's ready!"
Grabs a mug and pours a cup of tea.
"Huhhh, I hate this part…Isn't that right, Sawyer! Yesss, I hate drafting paperwork, yesss I do, yess I doo."
Woof!
"Where do I even start…alright,"
Reaches into a bag and picks up a recording.
"This seems like as good a place as any…whew, I really hope insurance accepts these…I'm not even sure I've accepted it yet…"

Presses play.

■ ■ ■

"President Donald J. Trump June15th Recording" turns on

Me: Mr. President. How are you? Thanks so much for joining me. Please have a seat…make yourself comfortable.

President Donald J. Trump: Well, it's not like I had much of a choice. I gotta say…I would have much more preferred we do this on my property—I have wayyy better accommodations…I mean I know you probably don't own the building but you gotta get your landlord to spruce this place up a bit…nice chandelier, maybe…You said it yourself. The goal is to make people feel comfortable, right?

Me: Speaking of comfortable, would you be uncomfortable if I called you Donald? I always want there to be a mutual sense of familiarity between my patients and me—

Donald: Ughh, "patients"…I don't like that word…makes me sound, I don't know…crazy or something, which I'm definitely not. Trust me, I've passed all of the tests. I'm more like a…client. Yeah! much better…this is just a deal I gotta get done…just like the thousands of others.

Me: But this is not a deal…business deals are voluntary. If you remember, these sessions were court-mandated, Donald. After the—

Donald: Okay, okay, we don't need to get into all of that. I mean you would not believe what charges Congress will come up with to attack me. It's incredible. They are sooo corrupt…it's ridiculous, but of course my lawyers ate up the lawsuit like they always do… I mean they're no Roy Cohn but they get the job done. No offense, you seem like a nice enough person, but I would have preferred to not have to waste my time with you…just saying. I'm 110 percent healthy…I mean, if anyone needs a shrink, it's Joe Biden! I'll tell you that! But it's not too bad. For what the charges were, I'll have a few sixty-minute conversations…just don't try to mess with my head with that shrink stuff!

Me: Well, you are in luck, because I'm not a psychiatrist. I'm a therapist. Actually a psychologist, if you want to be specific, but I specialize in different modalities.

Donald: So what happened…not good enough to be an actual doctor?

Me: I chose not to be a medical doctor.

Donald: Chose, huh, is that your fancy way of saying you weren't smart enough?

Me: Well, I did my undergrad at NYU, your old stomping grounds, if I recall…

Donald: Well, Queens, originally, but yeah, I have some properties around there—

Me: Plus, I acquired my Ph.D. at Brown University, so I would say I'm decently qualified.

Donald: I went to Wharton. That's an actual hard Ivy League school to get in to, and like my good friend Kanye always says, "I don't have a Ph.D., but I do have a Pretty Huge—

Me: Yes, I'm familiar with the saying.

Donald: Haha...plus, I'm rich, which is way more useful than degrees in the real world. But it would be just my luck, I get a second-rate head doctor to tell me about myself...Well, let me give you a heads up—there will be no laying down on couches or talking about feelings, alright? This may not be a business deal, but I'm calling the shots here. The deal is, I talk, and you listen, and that's if I feel like talking...don't start with any funny business. You basically work for me and I hate when employees waste my time.

Me: Donald...I don't work for you and we will only stop having sessions after I have signed off. Those were the terms your lawyer agreed to. If it helps, you can think of our time like a consultation, but instead of renovating a hotel or a golf course, YOU are the project and I'm just an outside contractor giving you advice. You can take it or leave it. Talk, don't talk. This "Donald J. Trump" tower will be as glorious as you want it to be...you are in the driver's seat because if this "project" goes bankrupt, you and only you will lose out.

Donald: You are more of a smart mouth than you are smart, you know that, right?

Me: Well, not as smart as you, I'm sure, so you should have nothing to worry about!

Donald: What is that?

Me: Oh, that blinking light behind me? That's the recorder...this session is being recorded.

Donald: Wowww, so Crooked Hilary, Nervous Nancy, and the Donkey Dems are back at it again...this is Obamagate all over again...who paid you off? Was it Ole Cryin' Chuck Schumer? He's been coming for me for years.

Me: No, this is a standard procedure for all my therapy sessions, plus it was in the legal agreement you signed. Do you remember? Sessions are recorded for my notes and for billing through your insurance, but I assure you these recordings are completely confidential.

Donald: I thought you said you weren't a doctor? So, there is no doctor-patient confidentiality and you could leak all of this.

Me: I'm required by law to make sure that doesn't happen. I just play this for my notes. You're free to be as open and forthcoming as you choose to be.

Donald: Openness use to be what Twitter was for before Twitter and other media outlets got infested with lies and misinformation from Antifa…or those Ticky Tackers.

Me: You mean Tik Tok…

Donald: Yeah, whatever! You know what I mean! Anyways, you wouldn't believe the malicious attacks…just filthy…I mean it's truly ridiculous.

Me: Well, why don't you tell me about these attacks.

Donald: Well, speaking of things manufactured in Chy-na…everything was fine before their virus destroyed the whole world…I mean, I saw this coming. Yup, since 1981…

Me: What happened in 1981?

Donald: That's when I published *The Art of the Deal*! Millions of copies sold…broke all kinds of records. I mean you should really read it.

Me: Did you write it yourself?

Donald: I don't see how that's relevant.

Me: Well, if you had a ghostwriter, then—

Donald: Anyway, the Chy-nese have been trying to sabotage America for soo long. With their despicable trade deals, which cheatin' Obama signed off on because, let's face it! He's probably not American, and now with their corona biological weapons, they will stop at nothing to get back at us for dropping the atom bomb on them!

Me: That attack was in Hiroshima and Nagasaki.

Donald: And?

Me: Those are cities in Japan.

Donald: Whatever. They are all friends, trust me…they are a threat to everybody, which I totally saw coming, which is why I tried to close the borders when all of the hippy liberals were complaining. And where are they now? Still want to give everybody a hug?

Me: But what do the Chinese have to do with you?

Donald: They ruined my beautiful economy!!! I mean everything was tremendous…unemployment was soo low…I mean, it was practically in the negatives…you could walk down the street and someone would beg you to work for them! It was just ridiculous how easy it was to get a job. Businesses were thriving, property values were booming…but, most importantly, there was tranquility, ya know? The country was doing very well, VERY well.

Me: Can you elaborate?

Donald: Well, no other president has been as successful as I have…No…One! I came in like the first week or something, the first day! I mean I don't have exact dates, but it was very quick…I got rid of that completely useless Obamacare that was just sucking up money like a broken vacuum. Then I cut all that red tape that was holding up businesses from being successful and moved all of the money earmarked for commie policies like universal healthcare to policies that we really need!

Me: And which policies did we "really need"?

Donald: Two words! Law and Order.

Me: Well that's three techn—

Donald: Listen, we are the number one country in the world…maybe ever! I mean I know we are top three at least…and countries want what we have, because we have the best of everything! I mean…education, food, technology, celebrities…and now, hehe, presidents!

Me: Is this why you told people to consider yourself the "Law and Order" president?

Donald: How do you know about that? You've been watching me, huh?

Me: I am prepared with all of my clients, but you are the President…I pay attention.

Donald: How could you not…I MAKE the news.

Me: So, is this why some of your executive orders in your first hundred days were …let's see here…"Enhance Public Safety in the Interior of the U.S.," "Border Security and Immigration Enforcement Improvements," and "Protecting the Nation from Foreign Terrorist Entry in the U.S"? To use the law to create order?

Donald: I just give people what they want. I mean, really, what they need. Without firm laws, there would be chaos. Without me, there would be chaos!

Me: Interesting…

Donald: What? What's interesting?

Me: Where does this paranoia come from? This need to feel safe? To feel protected? Do you often feel threatened?

Donald: I don't "FEEEEL" anything…I AM threatened…constantly.

Me: How so?

Donald: The lame-stream media attacks me every chance they get and when they can't find things to poke at, they make things up! It's true, but I don't mind, because when they come for me, I come back ten times, no, a hundred times harder! That's my problem with the left. They are such hypocrites. They cheat, lie, and make up things about everything I do, but they don't have the stones to get the job done themselves. I mean, as crooked as Hilary is, she really took the nads off Ole Wild Willy and I respect her for that, but that was literally the best the Dems could throw at me. A woman pretending to have the balls to go up against a man with a real pair. Now, this time around, they want to throw Average Joe at me, but it doesn't matter who they put up against me—they will get crushed when I'm done with him, because the simple truth is no one but me can get the job done! And they know this, so all they can do is discredit me! Lie on my name!

Me: So, when you say you are "threatened", do you mean by political opponents?

Donald: No, not just political opponents, by the disloyal and the ungrateful as well. You wouldn't believe it!

Me: Disloyal? Ungrateful? What do you mean by that?

Donald: So, I'm sure you've seen *The Apprentice*…

Me: I've definitely heard of it, but didn't have the pleasure—

Donald: Well, you really missed out, I mean it broke ALL of the records, millions of viewers…I mean probably the highest-watched show of all time…I don't know, I'd have to check the numbers but I know it was really high…NBC was really struggling before I got there…like really struggling and Jeff Zucker, the head of NBC at the time and whose job I single-handedly saved, goes to CNN and runs the most malicious lies about me since I've become president…Can you believe that? I mean, just disgusting. Even worse, one of the producers of *The Apprentice*, in the first season, he comes out after the whole Access Hollywood misunderstanding—

Me: The tape where you were joking with Billy Bush about grabbing women by the private parts…that misunderstanding?

Donald: Totally out of context by the way, but…uhh…anyway, he just takes his chance to pour gasoline all over the situation and tweets that I say things like that all the time!

Me: Why would he do that?

Donald: Because he's bitter he got fired! But without me, he wouldn't have a career! So where is the loyalty?

Me: Interesting…alright, that's our time for today. Let's pick this up next time.

Tape stops and picks up new tape

"Alright, fast forward…golfing, blah blah blah, ungrateful Melania… hmm…okay, here we go."

Presses Play of "President Donald J. Trump June 29th Recording"

Donald: Let me give you another one. There's really too many to count! It was like 2002, maybe 2003…I don't know…sometime in the early 2000s…and I had been crushing the New York real estate market. I mean, I was doing very well and so I decided to get into courses.

Me: Courses?

Donald: Yeah, golf courses. I mean, they were just slot machines and, of course, I was building really premium, high-quality courses.

Me: Okay…

Donald: So, low and behold, I offer my services to this small, kinda out-of-the-way town, Ranchos Palos Verdes.

Me: Ok, yes, in the Southern part of Los Angeles?

Donald: Right! Not L.A., but decent. But I generously offer to give them an upgrade on their crappy golf course that they just couldn't get done. I mean, their people were so incompetent, it was ridiculous. So, I come in and in practically no time, I mean, they had a mudslide like three years prior and, to be honest, it looked like the mudslide happened that afternoon. It was bad, I mean they were begging me, begging me to fix it up because the property value of all the residents was really low. But then, like a couple of years later, the school district gets real bold and squeezes me for rent while I'm building the course...can you believe that?

I mean, I'm from New York. I know Mafia guys...THIS was just amateur hour. I had just gone through a mayor from a course I was building in Briarcliff and he wanted to stiff me on the property taxes, but anyway, I told them to go to hell and that I would pay them for their share when the course was finished.

Me: So, what happened?

Donald: I took 'em to court! And I crushed them! I took the whole land and gave them a few mill for it. Real suckers.

Me: So, it looks like everything got resolved, then?

Donald: Are you crazy? No one tries to get one over me and gets away with it! Ugh...this guy was the worst. Milan Smith...just an obnoxious asshole that defended the school district.

Me: You mean Federal Judge Milan Dale Smith, Jr., on the ninth Circuit Court?

Donald: Yup, and he's still a sore loser! He tried to reject my terrorist ban!

Me: You mean your Muslim ban in 2017?

Donald: That's what I said...

Me: Hmmm, we'll have to unpack that later.

Donald: So, like I was saying, they were just being really ungrateful. Even when it was my land outright. One time, I wanted to put up Ficuses to block some ugly houses that were messing with my seaside views, and they had the nerve to complain about that, too! After all I was doing for them!

Then…now this really takes the cake…I wanted to put up a little American flagpole…like seventy feet.

Me: Seventy feet…wow.

Donald: I do it on all my courses. It's not a big deal. It's our flag, for Christ's sake. People should have paid me to do it! But, what a surprise! The guys that want terrorists in the country don't want an American flag! They had no respect for the flag and, worst of all, they had no loyalty!

So sometime later—I had to wait like two years or something super long like that—I was planning on building some houses and the city council said no again!

Me: And was that uncomfortable for you? Being denied…

Donald: Not really, I just did what I always do when someone comes after me…I hit back harder! I hit them with a 100-million-dollar suit just to remind them who was in charge. I think it was almost 2009 when they finally got a councilman with some sense…what was his name…smart guy….Oh yeah! Brian Campbell…really good guy. He wised up and gave me the houses, my name on the street, and the flagpole because he got what nobody else seemed to get: loyalty is always rewarded. And, most importantly, to not ever challenge me, because I will bury you! Just ask that joke of a President—Obama.

Me: President Barack Obama?? You never ran against him. I know you ran for President a few times before, but, if I recall correctly, as an independent in the 2008 election.

Donald: Yeah, I was just warming up to it. You know…feeling the terrain…I figured if my man Jesse Ventura could be governor of Minnesota after being a professional wrestler, anything was possible! This guy was an act at my casinos, and I thought to myself…he entertains in the building, but I OWN the building…so if he can be Governor…I can damn sure be the President!

Me: So, did he inspire you? An outsider with little leadership experience winning a political election?

Donald: I mean, I am very confident person. I have a lot of confidence, and people have been begging me to run since like '88, but no. It was that smug cheatin' Obama. He tried to embarrass me for saying what EVERYBODY was thinking but didn't have the gall to step up and say.

Me: To say what?

Donald: Are you even American!? Let's see the paperwork! I mean, I think it's a very fair question…I mean, Hawaii? Come on. Sounds fishy to me but, whatever. So he invites me to the Correspondents Dinner and just goes off for like half an hour about how I'm a joke and no one takes me seriously. That's all I needed. That was the moment. He threw the first stone, so I grabbed a bazooka! Called up Roger that night.

Me: Roger?

Donald: Roger Stone, yeah, a great guy, a real scrapper. Had to get him out of jail recently: payback for his loyalty. That's what I do for my friends. But anyway, after that dinner, the next day, we got to work and took his job. Now who's laughing…

Me: Well, his two terms were up—

Donald: I BURIEEDDD HIMMM! Him and all of his friends! And they never forgot it…because I won't let them. See, I'm like Julius Caesar! Their knives aim at my back, but they can never reach it because I keep my foot on their necks. Their arms are too short to box with me…

Me: So, now that you are president and arguably the most powerful man in the world, dissidence mustn't be as much of a worry anymore?

Donald: Are you kidding me? Did you see what that snake Mueller tried to pull off—"investigation"…more like a witch hunt.

Me: From my understanding, the charges for "collusion" were very serious.

Donald: It's just more conspiracies the Dems cooked up. They are all as rotten as it gets…believe me…they're all corrupt, especially their leader, Obama. That's why I only surround myself with the respectful ones—the loyal ones.

Me: Interesting…so is there anybody you feel like you can trust?

Donald: Of course! Take my son-in law—

Me: You mean your senior advisor, Jared Kushner?

Donald: I don't know what his title is but, yeah, Jared—great guy. Comes from good real estate money in New Jersey. It's not Manhattan but, still, a tough market…went to Harvard, too…real clever.

Me: Certainly, a lot of overlap.

Donald: Only difference is that he is a Jew and after that whole Charlottesville mess, you know with the Confederates and the instigators, the lame-stream media started saying I hated Jews, because, you know, some of my supporters are traditional with their values…but I'm thinking: "Are you crazy? My son-in law is a Jew! I love Israel! They are our people on the ground over there!" Best part, though, I didn't even have to tell Jared…the next day, he released an article setting the record straight.

Me: Wow…that must have been tough for him to support a base that is openly anti-Semitic.

Donald: HE ISS LOYALLL! HE GETS ITTT! You are with me or against me and if you are with me, you will win because I. ALWAYS. WIN.

That's what's so annoying. If people just got out of my way and let me do what it takes without questions, I would lead this country to prosperity. I will Make It Great. I've made things great so many times before. All they need to do is not question me, be loyal, and, frankly, grateful they have someone like me—someone with the chops to get it done. Not everybody can take it, but I can. Been doing it all my life.

Me: So this feeling behind "Make America Great"…is not "Greatness" in terms of equal access to great opportunities or equal access to great resources, but more a time where everybody stays in their "place"…where everybody is "loyal" and "obedient" to the ones that "win." Is that about right?

Donald: Exactly. Winners rule the world!

Me: Interesting. Something to consider though, is that this sort of perverse nostalgia…this longing for a grander, more pure, and more fundamental time…is not a new sentiment.

Donald: Yeah, I know. Had to copyright it from the first Bush and Reagan…decent presidents but I took it to another level.

Me: Haha, no…I mean further back than that. Like Francesco Petrarca in fourteenth century Florence, or maybe you know him as Petrarch…

Donald: Never heard of him.

Me: Right, so Petrarch used to describe this need to return to the "Old" Age of Ancient Greek greats like Cicero, Plato, and Pythagoras in order to escape the "evil" and "wretched fate" of his current time—the Middle Ages.

Donald: I mean, that was a depressing time…before America came through and dominated.

Me: But, doesn't this quote sound familiar to the America you describe now? The feeling that the current age is so full of corruption and destruction that we must return to the purity of some bygone era of greatness.

Donald: Okay, so you've read a few books. What's your point?

Me: This sentiment of returning to a previous time of "progress" seems to always center around American, European, or Greco-Roman cultural or imperial dominance over the rest of the world. So when you say, "winners rule the world," are you talking about these types of "winners"?

Donald: I mean, you can't argue with the results—look at the last five hundred years or so. We've been killing it!

Me: Historically, quite literally—

Donald: We are dominators! The world is better because America and Europe have been on top! Most of the world would still be in huts and wiping their asses with leaves if it wasn't for us. The world needs our leadership. It's in everybody's best interest.

Me: So, the consequential loss of culture, independence, and, sometimes, life is in colonized countries' best interest? I don't know if people of color would agree with that.

Donald: Listen, don't blame me! I'm just calling it how it is. There is a social order to things. Darwin talks about it and he was a scientist! Some people are just stronger than others. It's a fact! The strong ones are the winners.

Me: And these "winners" would keep winning if the "losers" just respected this hierarchy?

Trump: You're finally listening…Problems come when the "losers" have a lack of respect for the "winners."

Me: When they are disobedient?

Trump: Yes! That's why I love Twitter…well, I used to before it started crossing me. I more like the idea of it, you know? I can attack directly when people get out of line. Everything would be so simple if everybody were happy in their place but, now, everybody is trying to challenge the rules. Challenge me!

Rioting on my streets! In front of my house! Looting, destroying…they are out of control! Did you see what they let the NBA players do? Kneel during our beloved National Anthem! Paint that symbol of hate across the court! Across the streets! As if their lives matter more than any others. More than the honest, hard-working taxpayers across this country.

Me: So, are you implying that, if you support the Black Lives Matter movement, you are not a "hard-working taxpayer"?

Donald: The good ones are not causing trouble. Don't try to paint me as some racist! Whoopi already tried it with her dumb documentary.

Me: Whoopi Goldberg? What documentary?

Donald: That one with the New York thugs that got away with murder.

Me: Are you talking about *When They See Us*? The Netflix documentary about the "Central Park 5" that were wrongfully convicted for raping a white woman when they were kids? That was directed by Ava DuVernay, I believe.

Donald: Du-Bernie?...sounds like a foreigner just like Obama.

Me: She's not a—

Donald: She tried to say I was racist because I posted a letter about those thugs in the *New York Times* in like 1997 or something, saying that they should get the max. But it wasn't about race. It was about respect.

Me: Can you elaborate on what you mean by "respect"?

Donald: The 90s in New York City was a nasty place and bad people needed to know that if they even thought of causing chaos around me, in my city, I would destroy them.

Me: But, the defendants were kids….and they were found not guilty…

Donald: They were guilty of disobedience! You don't live anywhere near Central Park! I know because I've developed some amazing properties around there and trust me, they couldn't afford it! They need to go back to where they come from. They need to stay in their place!

But the disobedient are the ones that always feel most entitled. The weak feel entitled to what the strong have and that ungrateful mentality has kept America mediocre! Well, at least before me. America let the weak, the disobedient, the outsiders dilute what makes it great…but they won't win. I won't let them.

Me: I can't help but notice that your description of "obedience" and "hierarchy" seems to have an undertone of derision towards race and class. In your opinion, do you feel a hatred or intolerance to other races and cultures?

Donald: Are you calling me a bigot? You are out of your mind! I love the Blacks. And them and all the other minorities love me. Check the numbers! But, with everybody, there are good ones and bad ones and the difference is that the good ones know their place.

Me: What place is that?

Donald: Let me give you an example, my dear friend Robert…Umami or something—

Me: Robert Unanue, the CEO of Goya…he recently endorsed you for President, right?

Donald: Yeah, exactly! Him! Everybody is like, "Trump hates the Mexicans…Trump hates the beaners and that's why he is building a wall!…"

Me: Mr. Unanue is Puerto Rican…

Donald: What did I say? Anyway, I'm like, what are you talking about? I put my neck on the line promoting his products.

Me: Isn't that against the law?

Donald: I am the law! Anyway, his stocks go way up after that and he gets, like, so much press. Like, so much, it's ridiculous! But he's one of the good ones, so I help him out. Because he is LOYAL, and I respect a businessman. Not the ones sneaking into our country looking for a handout…no sir, not on my watch.

Who else? Who else??? Secretary of Housing, Ben Carson, Daniel Cameron—

Me: The Kentucky Attorney General that objected to charging the police officers in the Breonna Taylor shooting?

Donald: Yup—he knows how to tow the party line…Mitch McConnell really knows how to keeps his own under control…which reminds me! Of course, Tim Scott!

Me: The Republican Senator from South Carolina?

Donald: Yeah, him. He's Black and not the fake Black like Obama and Phony Kamala Harris. But the real Black…like the ones with no fathers and who sold drugs, probably…You know who I'm talking about. But yeah, so many support me because they know I'm going to take care of them…they know the order of things.

Me: Is this why you are such an ardent supporter of police? To maintain this "order"?

Donald: I mean blue lives matter and they have never mattered more than now with all of these Antifa disruptors and rioters destroying our country. Destroying our beautiful legacy! It's despicable…George Floyd didn't die so that these animals could cause chaos!

But that's what happens when you are the best. Everybody wants to take what you have…what they are too lazy or too incompetent to get themselves. I'm trying to protect us! The Brown rapists are trying to dig their way to our women, the lazy foreigners are trying to steal our jobs, the Chinese are trying to steal our money, the Muslims are trying to blow us up, and some of the Blacks just won't stop complaining. It's honestly exhausting and if I don't keep everybody under control, my gorgeous country won't return to the bombshell it once was.

Me: But for someone who always "wins," there seems to be a persistent feeling of threat and hostility—whether global, cultural, interpersonal—which is why you seem insistent on keeping everybody in their place, so that you can monitor or control their movements. But I'm curious…if you are so confident in yourself and your ability to lead, why the need to control people and things?

Donald: Well—

Me: It's something I want you to think about more than answer, but I do have a more direct question for you…Do you have any family history with people that struggle with mental health? Or suffer from any congenital disorders?

Donald: You better watch it…I don't know what you are trying to get at here, but—

Me: I'm sorry if you felt offended by my question. I only ask because, from what you have told me, you seem to be in a constant state of paranoia, hypersensitivity, anxiety…which can all present with bipolar symptoms and, in some cases, even schizophrenia if the presentation is—

Donald: I AM NOT CRAZY...YOU ARE CRAZY if you think that something is wrong with me!! You know how many tests they make me take? Physical tests, cognitive tests...I ace them all! I am a model specimen. My doctor always tells me you are so strong, so energetic. How do you do it? And I give HIM tips. I come from a long line of strong, healthy people. I mean, my dad passed when he was 94! Strong like an ox...all of us are.

Door slams...

Tape stops

"Oooh, my tea is getting cold. Need a refill. Alright, that's better."

Presses Play on "President Donald J. Trump July 13th Recording"

Me: So, I know our last session got a bit heated, but I wanted to revisit the topic of your health and your family. I am a healthcare professional, so it is a primary concern...

Donald: Alleged professional...

Me: Was the passing of your eldest brother, Fred, particularly difficult for you? The fact that he died at such a young age, in his 40s, I think it was? Especially in that fashion...alcoholism can be genetic and also can be comorbid with other mood—

Donald: Keep my brother's name out of your mouth!! Why do you want to bring up all of these deaths in my family? Why!? So you can get under my skin? Well, I'm telling you, doc, you got another thing coming if you think—

Me: Donald, my job is not to "get under your skin." I am not a psychiatrist, so I am certainly not trying to diagnose you, and even if I were, it wouldn't be fair for me to do so because of the prevalence of your public persona. If you are triggered by my inquiries, let's explore that. Set the record straight for me, because your niece, Mary, has made some strong declarations about your family and your upbringing…is there any truth to h—

Donald: She is a bitter, disloyal woman. I mean, I honestly feel for her, she had a tough go about it with how things went with Freddie and everything, but just because you got dealt a bad hand, that doesn't mean you attack your family. I mean, it's unforgivable! She made so many absurd accusations about us, but if you knew the full story—how great my family is—you would fall out of your seat! My grandfather, my dad… just incredible.

Me: Well, enlighten me.

Donald: Well, my dad and my grandmother would always tell me stories about his Pops when I was a kid. I never met him. He died long before I came around. My grandfather— Fredreich Trump, great guy, skin tough as leather…a grinder, knew how to put his nose to the ground and sniff out the best deals. He was German. He came from this small town called Kallstadt. Born into a good family with a good reputation. Known for the best wines, but anyway, he decides at like sixteen or something that he's too big for that town—really, all of Germany—and he left for America in like 1885. That's what people don't get. My grandparents were immigrants! Got no problem with immigrants, but not all of them are like my grandfather. He's one of the good ones. Maybe one of the best, actually! But he came with one suitcase and no English. Didn't make excuses…didn't ask for handouts…just went to work. He started out as just a barber! He was strategic. He laid low, stacked his money, and waited for the next big opportunity. Finally, after toiling in Manhattan for seven years, the national papers reported that some niners stuck gold out west. Grandpa played it smart though, you see. He didn't chase the gold because everybody was chasing the gold…there would be none left. He figured the people mining all day for gold gotta eat, gotta drink at some point, so he opens up his first restaurant in Seattle. He realized that the dining industry was the real gold mine!

Me: Did he have any experience with restaurants? I know his family made wines and he was doing odd jobs in Manhattan, but owning a restaurant seems like a big undertaking.

Donald: Not for a Trump. We don't need lots of experience; we just succeed! So, like I was saying…he hit the jackpot with his restaurant but he couldn't keep it under control— cooks fighting, customers gambling. So he goes to Monte Cristo because Rockefeller opened up a mining station there, but in order to get there he had to carry all of his supplies by foot through Dead Horse Trail in the Canadian Rocky Mountains! Do you know why they called it Dead Horse Trail?

Me: Because of all the dead horses…

Donald: You betcha! It was such a rough terrain, horses couldn't survive the trek. But check this out! Not only did my grandpa survive the journey, he managed to open up a pop-up restaurant serving horse burgers! See, Grandpa learned a lesson that he taught my dad and that my dad eventually taught me—there is ALWAYS profit in tragedy!

So after the restaurant, Grandpa Fredreich arrived at Monte Cristo but all of the gold was wiped out. So, the miners left to pan gold in a thriving town called Bennet. Grandpa followed the miners to Bennet where he builds the first in a long line of fabulous Trump hotels…it was really a thing of beauty. But get this, one day, for practically no reason, all of the miners decide to bail on Bennet and switch towns again! They move to another town called White Horse down the river. So what did my Pops do? Give up and go home? Quit? Nope! He literally packs up the whole building up, puts it on a raft and sails it downstream to White Horse Just incredible! And he made a lot of money too…like a lot! Everything was rolling for him because he always found a way to give the people what they wanted—broads, booze, beds, you name it! He did whatever it took.

Me: It sounds like your grandfather was creating quite a life for himself, why didn't he stay on the West Coast?

Donald: The feds got jealous that they weren't getting a piece of the action, so they came in and shut everything down. I tell ya, If the government would just stay out of the way of good business, this country would be way better off…but anyways…he made a lot of money and so he figures it's time to cash out and go back home to Germany, and would you believe that the Bavarian government wouldn't let him back in!Isn't that ridiculous! Here comes this wealthy guy who has proven himself and they don't want him back in. I just don't understand it but they cited some technical rule, missing military service or something. It doesn't matter. All you need to know is that it was more government interfering with good businessmen for no reason. But he is a winner, so he adapted. He took his new wife, my grandmother Elizabeth, and went back to Manhattan to open up a barbershop-full circle! After a few years, he combines his profits from the barbershop with money from his savings and starts buying properties…I told ya, I come from a long line of greatness. I mean, sure, he had his vices like everybody else. He liked the bottle, but that didn't do him in. The influenza got him in '18, but my dad—

Me: Frederick Christ Trump, right?

Donald: Right. my granddad is Friedrich and my dad is Frederick or just Fred senior.

Me: Got it.

Donald: So, like I was saying, my dad, who was the oldest of three, picked up the business when he was just 12!

Me: That is a young age to be the man of the house.

Donald: It was in his blood, our blood. Didn't even need formal training or schooling. He was drawing blueprints, building garages, and by seventeen he was building his first house! So, he took over the family business. He was doing very well, extremely well, but in his early 20s, I think, when the Great Depression hit, America went tits up! But he is a Trump! And he learned the same lesson his father learned with the horse burgers on dead horse trail…one man's tragedy is a businessman's treasure.

Me: How so?

Donald: My father was a really smart guy, like really smart…probably a genius. He made all of these connections with different politicians around the city and when Roosevelt created all of these housing contracts after the Great Depression, my dad ate them all up! Because of the economic depression, competing businesses were busting left and right, so my dad took advantage. He was an animal! The *Daily Eagle*, this old school newspaper but pretty big for its time, called him the Henry Ford of housing. Can you believe that? He was as big as the guy who invented cars! That was around the time he met my mom, Mary—Mary Macleod was her maiden name, she is from the Isle of Lewis—

Me: That is in the U.K., right?

Donald: Yeah, you know your stuff, doc! Anyway, my dad liked her because she was a fighter: fearless! Just like my granddad. But also, just a very nice woman…so they would roll around in Rolls Royces and furs and he just became the ultimate showman. Everybody loved him. So they started to have kids…to keep the legacy going.

Me: Especially on June 14th right? 1946…

Donald: Haha that's right, should be a national holiday really…best thing to happen to America was me being born.

Me: So what was your childhood like? From your perspective…because Mary, your niece, describes it as pretty abus—

Donald: Mary doesn't even know what she's talking about! It's not like she was there. She's only heard rumors and secondhand accounts, which she has little context for. I mean, we lived in the biggest house on the block…everybody knew who we were!

Me: But Mary, in her book, describes your home, particularly your father, as emotionally and psychologically abusive…your mother absent and preoccupied with post-partum complications after the birth of her fifth child, your brother Robert. Are you saying that these factors had no effect on you?

Donald: My dad was a no-nonsense guy and he was building an empire, but he's always been there for me…

Me: But she describes you as a bully, violent, impatient with other children. Is it true that you once threw something at a teacher and that is what prompted you to be sent to military school?

Donald: First of all…she totally had it coming! And second of all, I wasn't a bully, I was tough—a leader—and I got sent to the New York Military Academy because my dad found a switchblade in my bag that I forgot to hide. He honestly overreacted. It wasn't a big deal, but, honestly, going to the military academy wasn't half bad at all…I learned a lot there.

Me: Like what?

Donald: Well, for one, I was a total stud: star football player, baseball player. I dominated on and off the field. If someone had a problem with me, I wasn't afraid to show how fast my hands were, but you know, that's typical boy stuff, especially in the military. It's good for boys to get out some aggression every once in a while.

Me: Sounds like you were using physical abuse to distract from the emotional abuse.

Donald: There is no room for feelings in the military! Only the mission! General Dobias taught me that.

Me: Who is General Dobias?

Donald: General Theodore Dobias, a really tough guy; he ran "F" company and showed me the ropes…taught me a lot. He used to have these quotes all over the hallways and I never forgot them, like "when the great scorer comes to write against your name, he writes not whether you won or lost but how you played the game." Good stuff, but my favorite, hands down, was this one: "winning isn't everything, it's the only thing." You do whatever you need to do to complete the mission…to win.

Me: So this preoccupation you have with "winning" came from him? Dobias?

Donald: No, not exactly. My dad used to tell me that "we are killers, we are kings."

Me: What does that mean?

Donald: It means winning is in our blood. You are either born with it or you aren't.

Me: So why do you think the rest of your family hasn't enjoyed the type of notoriety you have?

Donald: Well, blood will get you started, but it's not enough. My dad's reverend—Reverend Norman Vincent Peele—wrote this book called *The Power of Positive Thinking*. You gotta read it, doc, might help you become better at practicing medicine.

Me: Again, I am a psychologist…but, nevertheless, why was this book so important?

Donald: Because he was right! He said if you think positively enough about anything, absolutely any situation—no matter how bad it is or how unprepared you are—it will turn out ok! That positive thinking is the key to success and success is the closest way to becoming godly… because you are relying on faith. Since I heard him speak, my faith in myself has been unwavering…that's why, when Freddie failed at the business, I knew I had what it took to take the family business to a whole other level. So after I finish military school and get my degree from Wharton…passed with flying colors—

Me: But Mary said that you allegedly had someone take the SAT test for you to get in.

Donald: I'm only going to tell you this one more time doc…she is bitter and a bitch! I hate to say it, but it's true. You can't believe anything she says, so stop bringing her up or I swear I will end these sessions and your practice! You do not want to get on my bad side.

Me: Ok, then, we won't bring up Mary again…let's just focus on you.

Donald: Good answer! So, like I was saying…I had my sights on the major leagues, the big times…Manhattan real estate.

Me: So, is this what you meant by "your dad was always there for you"? He kind of handed you the keys to the Trump Corporation?

Donald: Well, yeah but I upgraded everything! My dad was really successful…I mean, tremendously successful but he couldn't get out of Brooklyn and Queens. I wanted to go after the major clients…upper crust, not the bottom-feeders in Trump Village.

Me: Wasn't there a lawsuit where Trump Village was sued for discriminatory practices towards renters of color?

Donald: Completely bogus!…no cred—

Me: But you ended up settling, I believe, so there must have be—

Donald: That was just a big misunderstanding, which is why I had to get out of the second-rate boroughs. You gotta understand—it was the mid-seventies! The whole city was ruined by politicians by people wanting handouts and all of these food stamp programs. Crime was everywhere! There was a garbage strike, so there was literal filth in the streets because Beame laid off—

Me: Are you referring to former New York Mayor Abraham Beame?

Donald: Yup, he canned like thousands of police officers…it was crazy. In the fifties, the city used to be called Fun City and then, in like two decades, it became Fear City…I mean, you couldn't go outside, but like my dad said, one man's tragedy…

Me: Another man's treasure, right?

Donald: You got it…hehe. That's how I got my first deal…I remember like it was yesterday…the Commodore.

Me: Commodore? What is that?

Donald: 109 East 42nd Street! Right straight dab in the middle of Midtown…beautiful piece of real estate that I restored…of course, it's not called that anymore. You may know it as the "Grand Hyatt."

Me: How did you manage that?

Donald: So Beame, right—poor sap—he was tucking his tail between his legs and just wagging his tongue; begging everyone to bail him out because his welfare programs were bankrupting the city! He went to the Governor, the Treasury Department, and even old President Ford… everybody! And they wouldn't give him a lick because they didn't trust him, and I don't blame 'em. Politicians need to stay out of the way of good business. But anyways, he was desperate to turn things around.

Me: But you must have been in your twenties at this time? Did you have a relationship with Mayor Beame?

Donald: No, no, my dad and him went way back, so het set up the deal…but I closed it!

Me: How so?

Donald: Well, the way I figured…I'm taking all the risk. I'm doing all the leg work because a good hotel can't just be made well…people gotta want to come! And with the city the way it was, I was the one who could market it the right way, who could make it glamorous, because I thought positively about the Commodore's success so it became a success. See, Reverend Peale's stuff works!

Me: I understand…

Donald: So, I figure…if I'm doing the city a favor, they shouldn't tax me? Right? If you mow someone's lawn, should you have to pay them for a glass of water if you get thirsty? No! They should be taking you out to lunch! On their knees thanking you that you saved their shitty yard! So Ole Beame gave me a little fight, but with my lawyer Roy Cohn behind me, I got the deal done.

Me: "Deal done?"

Donald: Yeah, forty years, no property taxes…I think it was the least they should do.

Me: Well, that is quite an achievement.

Donald: Yeah, but that was just the beginning. I needed something better, something bigger. Something to remind everybody who was running things in Manhattan. I needed the Trump Tower and I needed it on Park Avenue…so I got Barbara.

Me: Barbara? So, a woman?

Donald: Yeah, Barbara Res—people try to say that I hate women. I love women! No one was hiring women in construction. No one! But I did…I love women. But anyway, she was tough, gritty…I like that. I like people who can get the job done…her and Artie—Artie Nusbaum—the construction manager of HRH. We got to work and created the finest hotel In America, hands down…thing of beauty.

Me: So, did Mayor Beame give you the same tax abatement as the Commodore renovation?

Donald: Well, Beam was out. It was the eighties. Reagan was in office and he got it. He understood the value of good business, but Ed Koch came in as the mayor and he was the most obnoxious guy…I mean, just the absolute worst.

Me: Why was he the worst?

Donald: Because he got in my way. Well, he tried to stiff me on the tax abatements but eventually, like anybody in my way, he gave in. Yeah, the eighties were great, man…really great. I got into casinos in '84 and opened the Plaza…then, boom! Hit them with the Trump castle! I mean, I was unstoppable…

Me: Well, until the Taj Mahal, right?

Donald: The Taj was a learning experience…I don't really consider it a failure because I learned a lot from that experience. My eyes probably got a little too big for my stomach, but the way the jackals came after me was just horrendous…absolutely despicable…

Me: What do you mean…"came after you?"

Donald: Well, I was getting grief over the tax abatements, which I still don't get, and then this guy…what was his name…oh, yeah! Marvin Roffman. Worked at the *Journal* and was yapping his gums, telling everybody that the Taj was going to fail…before it even opened! I mean, what type of bull is that?

Me: But wasn't he ultimately right?

Donald: That's not the point! If you think negatively about something, you will get negative results—and, by the way—who is he? What had he accomplished? What gives him the right to embarrass me? But when people say something false, I attack those people…I correct them. That's what happened with this guy named Wallach. Abraham, I think was his name…he worked for First Capital at the time. He tried to hop on the slander bandwagon and, after Roy dropped a lawsuit on his boss's head, he wised up. And I ended up hiring him, heh.

Me: Why would you hire someone you felt "slandered" you?

Donald: So that he never forgot his place. See, when things weren't working out with Ivana, my first wife, and the Taj, the sharks thought they smelled blood in the water. But I learned something my dad never figured out: anybody will believe anything, if you're the only one telling the story…

Me: What do you mean, "something your dad never figured out?"

Donald: So, after World War II—around the time I was born—the government had this program to build houses for veterans. You know, for the G.I. Bill and everything. So he gets the contract…Levittown, Brooklyn, Queens…a bunch of suburb jobs, and sends the bill to the government for goods and services needed to get the job done. Well, he figures a way to get the job done with half of what they give him and he pockets the rest…which by the way was not illegal…it was just smart! Anyway, Eisenhower gets upset, mostly because he got outsmarted. He made a whole big thing about it and made my dad testify in front of the Senate. On television! They found him innocent, of course, because he WAS innocent.

Me: So, that's great then…sounds like it all worked out?

Donald: Are you nuts? They ruined his reputation! Our reputation. The Trump name! It was worse than them putting him in jail! Listen, all a man has at the end of the day is his legacy…his name! And if you take that away from him, you might as well have killed him!

Me: So what does what happened to your father have to do with the Taj Mahal bankruptcy, your first divorce, and all of the bad press?

Donald: Because, Doc, my dad didn't control the story. And he paid the price! When someone attacks me, I discredit them. When the tabloids ran a story about Ivana, I gave them a better one. When my creditors tried to shake me down for my debt, I told them what they wanted to hear. See, that's why winning is everything because everybody believes the winner…so I do everything in my power to keep winning. They said the Wollman Rink couldn't be built—I got it done in three months! They said I was broke, I turned the Trump Corporation global! They said I couldn't be President…well, we all know how that ended up. I ALWAYS end up on top.

Me: Fascinating….

Donald: I know, right. I'm pretty unbelievable.

Tape stops

Gotta pee…gotta pee! Whew, that's better…Alright, where is that next one?

Presses Play of "President Donald J. Trump July 27th Recording"

Me: Last session I said I was fascinated—

Donald: How could you not be?

Me: Ha! No, Donald. What's fascinating was that I was leaning towards a genetic disorder but after everything you've shared with me, I think a personality disorder might be more fitting…perhaps megalomania…narcissism, certainly a God complex…perhaps sociopath—

Donald: What the hell are you talking about? Did you not listen to a word I said?

Me: I've actually listened to every word you've said…wrote down some notes, too, so that I wouldn't forget…if you don't mind…

Donald: Ohh, this will be rich; I'd love to hear this.

Me: Well, when I really break down the patterns of your narrations, I find that you rely heavily on five primary modes of communication…

One: When you feel provoked, attacked or embarrassed, like in my recount of your niece Mary's depiction of your childhood, you respond with vitriol to mask your vulnerability in order to evade accountability or contrition. That is to say…you counter-attack uncomfortable narratives about you unapologetically, regardless of the validity of that narrative.

Two: You use hyperbole—

Donald: Hyper…what? what does that mean?

Me: Hy-per-bowl-e…It means that you use a form of exaggeration, a grandiose form of embellishment, to mask your insecurities and uncertainties. Like when you talk about your fitness as a president, for instance, but also incidentally, to provoke confirmation bias.

Donald: Confirmation bias?

Me: Confirmation bias is the tendency to search for, interpret, or recall information in a way that confirms or supports one's prior beliefs or values. Like in the case of your failed business ventures or bankruptcies, you use hyperbole as a sort of aggressive peacocking. A way to flap your metaphorical feathers at an opponent in order to intimidate perceived opposition but also, concurrently, to invoke a feeling of confidence and awe in the observer witnessing the confrontation.

Donald: Alright that's enough of this bull—

Me: That actually brings me to my third one: avoidance. When you get caught off-guard in a conversation, you evade the question or comment as a way of stalling in order to avoid outright retreat, concession, or submission to a vulnerable position in the debate or conversation. In this way, you can maintain control of the tempo or direction of the conversation, because if the conversation veers towards an objective truth or conventionally accepted reality, it might be too difficult for you to accept.

Donald: I'm not running from anything…I'm correcting your dumb pseudo—

Me: Four: You use dismissal as a way of regaining power. As a way to bargain or negotiate leverage in a conversation. It's your way of avoiding cognitive dissonance or psychological discomfort, at least long enough for you to collect a counter argument or an exit strategy.

And, finally, truisms, one of the most salient aspects of your speech.

Donald: What are—

Me: Truisms are statements that are obviously true and don't add anything constructive to a conversation. You will say something with nominal value like, "winners win and losers lose," and apply it in a logically incoherent way. It cannot be disproven because it is inherently descriptive and thus doesn't actually apply to the nature of the subject, just its presentation, which is inherently subjective and, if needed, can be applied retroactively. Like when you said, "That's why I banned the borders, because I knew before everyone else that the Chinese virus was a threat!" Biological viruses are an obvious natural threat. That statement is a truism and you applied this truism ex post facto to justify a policy that was, in all actuality, intended to be xenophobic.

Donald: You still don't get it, doc. Things don't need to make sense to you or anybody else for that matter. Whatever I say doesn't have to be logical or rational or whatever the hell you just said because if I want something to be true, it will be true…if I want it to be real, it will be real. This is the power of positive thought. "Logic" is irrelevant. As long as I want something to make sense bad enough, the logic will follow. It's been true all of my life! Look at the results! Every time I was bankrupt, I said I wasn't and then, after a while, I wasn't…all positive thinking. I'm just great. It's my destiny or something…

Me: You know who you remind me of…Aristotle.

Donald: That's the smartest thing you said this whole time. Great man…wise man…just like me.

Me: Aristotle once said that if you drop two objects at the same time, where one is ten times as heavy as the other, the heavier object will fall ten times faster.

Donald: Makes sense to me.

Me: Yes, it made sense to Aristotle, too, but the problem is that this theory is false. Isaac Newton discovered that an object's acceleration due to gravity is always constant regardless of weight. But strangely, Aristotle's followers, similar to your followers Donald, never felt the need to prove his theory. They just accepted it blindly.

Donald: That's the way it should be…why should leaders have to explain themselves?

Me: Because although he is one of the most influential figures in history, it is not necessarily because of his accuracy. For example, he thought that everything in the world was made out of five elements…water, fire, air, earth, and the aether—this transient nothingness that occupied outer space. He also thought that women were inherently inferior to men because men have sperm that is "hot and warm" and consequently gives them the virility and "fire" to lead, while women have "cold' and "wet" eggs that make them docile and meek.

Donald: I mean, that doesn't seem entirely wrong.

Me: But, in a sense, he was…wrong, that is. And this is problematic because Aristotle's writing has had profound influence on the way our culture views everything from Biology, Ethics, Metaphysics, Logic…just to name a few. Aristotle is also the same person that came up with the idea that the "civilized" mind—meaning any mind that was Greek—is inherently rational…logical.

Donald: See, you are contradicting yourself. You just said he was wrong about everything, but that sounds right to me! Americans are very rational…very civilized.

Me: But Americans' or any other individual's brain does not inherently operate with rationality. The brain works off of emotion, impulse, memory, and mostly subconscious percepts that give it an incomplete view of the world. So this idea that any one person can trust their untested and biologically fundamental "reasoning" skills leads to an instance where a well-known political leader, for instance, might ask people to, let's say, "ingest bleach," and people consider it without question. The person takes the descriptive value of your suggestion, "bleach cleans things…I want my body to be clean, that must make sense" and assume that the statement has come from a "rational" place. Why? Because we can assume most Americans have had access to some level of public education and thus have most likely studied any one of the subjects Aristotle has influenced: Psychology, Economics, Politics, etc. Aristotle has primed your audience to accept your declaration at face value even before they tested the validity of it. In turn, you view this acceptance as empirical proof of your statement's validity.

So, to put it plainly, you assume that if everybody accepts it, it must be true. It must be factual. But this phenomenon of Americans, Europeans… really any culture influenced by Romans or Greeks…defining their reality based off of ancient Greco-Roman philosophy leads to a generally misleading understanding of how the natural world objectively operates.

Donald: So says you…that's just a matter of opinion! I don't think there is anything wrong with how I think or how my forefathers thought. If it's good enough for a textbook, it's good enough for me! And why are you bringing up LITERAL ancient history? What's done is done…what the hell does this have to do w—

Me: Because, Donald, your unfounded confidence, your constant need to overcompensate, and your delusions of grandeur and superiority are very consistent with my prognosis. It's actually quite textbook, given your relationship with your parents. But what is profoundly more interesting to me is how our society's ontological constructs have not only rewarded your philosophies but how, for so long, America has enabled the delusion that your view of the world is in anyway objectively credible.

Donald: Onto—what? What are you even talking about? You're using a lot of big words but not really saying anything.

Me: Ontological means the basic ideas behind what exists and what doesn't, what's real and what's not. Our language shapes not just what we say but how we think about the world…and most of America's language and subsequent view of the world is shaped by pre-Copernican philos—

Donald: Speak English! Pre-Capricorn? What are you saying? I'm a Gemini.

Me: Ha! no…Pre-Coper-ni-cus…as in before "Copernicus."

Donald: What is Copernicus?

Me: Nicolaus Copernicus was an astronomer from the sixteenth century. He was one of the first people to model a universe where the earth revolved around the sun. Before then, much of the western world was geo-centric…which means that they thought the earth was the center of the universe.

Donald: Why does that matter? People make mistakes all the time… not a big deal.

Me: It's a big deal because this sort of distorted belief about humanity's importance relative to the rest of the universe shaped how the Greeks and Romans viewed the natural world and, in turn, influenced the language they used to describe it.

Think about it…you and I are speaking English and more than two billion people, roughly a quarter of the whole world, speaks English. Like French, German, Spanish, Italian and all the other Romance languages, our language and most commonly spoken languages come from Latin or Greek. You know who spoke Latin and Greek? You guessed it! The Romans and the Greeks.

Donald: I wasn't really trying to guess, but—

Me: You mentioned earlier how you were a Gemini, right? Well, you're referring to Astrology.

Donald: So, you are going to tell me that Astrology is fake, too? It's taught in school! It's the study of the stars. People learn it all the time!

Me: That's Astron-omy…Astrology doesn't have any modern scientific basis. Let me give you an example. Are you familiar with the term "retrograde" as in "Mercury is in retrograde." This phrase was coined inaccurately because the Greeks thought that Mercury actually orbited the earth with reverse momentum.

Donald: Soooo…what's the problem?

Me: The problem is that it doesn't. It just looks like it does because of how fast the earth is orbiting around the sun in relation to Mercury. Here's a simpler example. You know the words "sun-set" and "sun-rise"? Before Copernicus, Greeks thought that the sun actually rose from below a horizon and, at the end of the day, fell below the horizon. Disappearing out of sight, while the earth stood still. In reality, the sun sets because the earth rotates around its axis and completes a turn every twenty-four hours. We use these words and ideas in a matter-of-fact way…in an objective way…but they are really just incomplete assessments of what the Greeks didn't have the tools to confirm. Even beyond the words we use, the way our society constructs sentences is misleading.

Donald: Maybe Sleepy Joe, no one can tell what the hell this guy is talking about half of the time.

Me: No, EVERYBODY or, at least, every English speaker…think about it…for a statement to be considered a complete sentence…you have to have…

Donald: A point? Something you don't have right now?

Me: A subject, a verb, and a complete thought…but, more importantly, for the thought to be declarative in the active voice, the subject has to come first. Plus, the subjects are always nouns…people, places, things. Ringing a bell?

Donald: Anndddd...?

Me: If the prerequisite for a "complete" thought is that it has to have a noun in it and most correct sentences require you to start the sentence with a subject, then every thought you've ever had about yourself would start essentially with an "I."

Donald: I...want this joke of a therapy to be over...

Me: Thank you for the great example...here is another. "I want to walk with you and see the birds in the forest." Since the complete thought starts with "I," the speaker has no choice but to psychologically place more value to the "I" than the "you" or the "birds" or the "forest"! If you have thousands of conscious thoughts a day and perhaps even millions of subconscious thoughts a day, then your brain is profoundly more susceptible to shaping your understanding of the world around you—around "I"—because every thought starts with "I." "I," the subject, becomes more salient than any other piece of information in that thought.

Donald: You need to feel like you are more important than anyone or anything else...that's how you become more important than anyone or anything else.

Me: The issue is that you are not, objectively. No one person is in relation to the rest of the world and the fact that humans, not unlike yourself, see themselves as universally more important than any other part of nature leads us to devalue everything that we don't psychologically associate with "I." For instance, if the earth's temperature is rising, it is easy to disregard because it has nothing to do with "I." If I'm American and a Syrian town has been catastrophically destroyed, the cognition of "Syrian" has no relational value to "I." If someone dies from COVID-19, but you have no experience with them, then you inherently value their life less because they have no empirical effect on "I." "I" ALWAYS comes first.

But this is not necessarily the case with all languages or all people, of course. Many East Asian languages construct sentences with context or setting first before gradually narrowing to the subject, which is a sort of reminder of an individual's place relative to other people and, frankly, to everything else in the world.

Donald: Well, what don't you just move to China since you love them so much…see how well you can understand a damn thing they say!

Me: I'm not suggesting that any one culture is better than another. I'm simply breaking down why your communication style—the vitriol, avoidance, hyperbole—is exacerbated by the fact that you live in a culture that is not aware of its conflated self-importance. That's why it's even more important for you to stay vigilant about what you say and, consequently, the thoughts you generate about yourself.

Donald: My "culture" doesn't "think" it's important…my culture, my country IS important…We are number one, the best in the world.

Me: Hmmm.. you would consider yourself as White correct? A White man?

Donald: And proud of it!

Me: So when you say your "culture," you are referring more specifically to White culture then, correct?

Donald: I mean, sure. If you want to be specific.

Me: Do you know one of the definitions of white?

Donald: Awesome, probably?

Me: Free from moral impurity. Innocent—marked by upright fairness.

Donald: Sounds about right to me.

Me: And where in "your country," as you put it, do most Americans originate from?

Donald: Uhhhh…from pilgrims?

Me: Europe! And do you know what the root word Eu means? It's Greek for good, well, true, and genuine.

Donald: Okaayyy.

Me: Your "culture" and your "country," as you put it, have defined themselves by what they want them to be instead of what they have historically been. And, since World War II, your culture and your country have used capitalism, democracy, and marketing to imbue the world with your language, your holidays, your calendars, your movies, your music, and your stories to create a sense that your culture is destined to be at the center of this world. It is this perception that creates a sense of authority and righteousness that serves only to distract from a deeper and more painful uncertainty or doubt…that you and your culture may not entirely be what you have defined themselves to be.

Donald: Bu—

Me: Hold, that thought. I was told you were on a schedule…

Tape stops

"I think this is the last one…only one way to find out…"

Presses Play of "President Donald J. Trump August 10ᵗʰ Recording"

Me: Hello Donald, how ar—

Donald: You've got it all backwards, doc. Everybody in the world thought we were great, because we are. We just turned their love for us into profit! Nothing wrong with that…just good business!

Me: Alright, let's jump right in, then. That's certainly an interesting theory…may I assume you watched cartoons growing up?

Donald: Back when they were good. When they weren't trying to make every single Disney princess a different color…I mean, it's ridiculous… what are they trying do? Get through the whole Crayola box? Princesses, princes, kings, and queens are from medieval British stories…and you can't say that's racist…that's just a fact! People are always trying to take my culture—I'm telling you. Because it's great…because they want it.

Me: Another interesting theory. An alternative theory is that these "stories" that you say everybody else wants are something your culture wants, too. It would be nice to think that damsels in distress were patiently and coquettishly waiting in castles for brave and valiant men to fight dragons for them. To kiss or whisk them away to a castle, but in the Middle Ages, most knights slaughtered and killed people at will. There was constant fighting because they were perpetually drunk. Due to poor water quality, they had to drink beer instead of water. The sewage system was so bad that most people literally slept in filth. The average life expectancy was the late twenties, early thirties. Young women didn't stumble upon a handsome prince in their late teens and early twenties; they were often forced to marry as early as the age of six.

Donald: What do you have against watching fairy tales? Oh, I get it! You were too busy reading books…like a nerd.

Me: So, are you saying that reading books is bad?

Donald: You are twisting my words. I read all the time…great reader…one of my favorite books is, *Where the Wild Things Are*.

Me: So, the book where an insolent Max throws a temper tantrum instead of accepting accountability for his actions and then travels to a far-away land just to avoid said accountability. Then, in order to validate his behavior and self-worth, Max becomes the "king" of the savage "wild things," only to return home with tales of how he narrowly avoided his own death despite his attempts to tame the wild and tempestuous creatures…that book?

Donald: I'm not sure we are talking about the same book…you are making it sound so complicated. It's a pretty delightful, straightforward book.

Me: We are talking about the same book. And if you replace Max with Christopher Columbus, Vasco de Gama, Ponce de Leon—really, any European explorer—and substitute "wild things" for the Incas, the Mayans, the Native Americans…you've essentially have a watered-down, euphemized, and infantilized revisionist history of colonialism.

Donald: Ugghh…what? You're reading way too much into this. No wonder you are a shrink…you think way too much.

Me: What I'm trying to illustrate to you, Donald, is that ever since America has become a superpower, we have used capitalism, marketing, and selective storytelling to created an image of American culture as infallible and superior to everyone else. Entrepreneurs then target the most vulnerable populations…the ones that are psychologically most susceptible to internalizing myths—children.

Donald, you were born in 1946, right after the deadliest war in history. Your generation never knew of a world were America wasn't considered a superpower and you, your generation, and the succeeding generations that have been raised and influenced by the baby boomers have internalized these myths, these sanitized revisions of history, as fact since they have not witnessed any empirical evidence to counter these narratives. But just because America, Europe, or any society in western culture controls the narrative, it doesn't mean the narrative is actually true. The accomplishments of a culture don't exist in a vacuum. The achievements and innovations of any culture usually come from a collective global effort.

Donald: Now, that's just a lie, a bald-faced lie! My ancestors were like my actual father and my grandfather…great men. They didn't need any help. They just got the job done. They built their empire with their bare hands!

Me: Your mother…Mary…you said her maiden name was Macleod, right?

Donald: Yeah, so what?

Me: Macleod is a traditional Scottish name, and do you know what a staple of the Scottish diet is?

Donald: Hehe…whiskey?

Me: Potatoes! And do you know where potatoes come from? Peru, Chile, and northwestern Bolivia.

Donald: Different foods come from a lot of places…what's your point?

Me: The reason why the potato famine in nearby Ireland was the cause of mass starvation and widespread disease for four consecutive years is because the potato is not just an average crop. The potato is not only rich in carbohydrates but is also notoriously low-maintenance. It doesn't need much fertilizer or soil to grow and can grow almost everywhere. If the Incas hadn't introduced the potato to the Europeans, and, subsequently, your mother's ancestors, their daily regimen of nutrition would have stayed at a very low level. The soil and climate of the United Kingdom is not a fertile land for growing a variety of nutritious food. More potatoes mean more energy. More energy means more strength and more strength means better health. Better health equals more time, more ability to innovate, to think, and to improve life conditions. So without the potato and the Incan agricultural techniques that came with it, your mother might not have even made it to America.

Donald: Don't you dare talk about my mother! I told you to watch your mouth about my family!

Me: What I'm saying is that much of European thinkers and inventors directly or indirectly benefited from the spoils of colonized agriculture. Europeans acquired much of what they learned about agriculture from enslaved African agriculturalists. Additionally, Europeans received an increase in the production of goods like tobacco, cotton, tea, and sugar produced in enslaved colonies in the Americas. But it wasn't just agriculture they benefited from; it was also trade. Corporations and traders became rich off the global expansion of trade…a market they could only monopolize by the support of local trading posts in Africa and Asia. Most of the famous Renaissance painters, inventors, and thinkers were usually sponsored by the church or a rich Italian family like the Medicis. The Medicis acquired most of their wealth by trading with Africa and Asians along the Mediterranean and this cross-cultural pollination transported ideas along with goods. The system of numerals we use for the basis of mathematics was created by the Arabs. The formula for creating gunpowder that Europeans used to forcibly take over the world was created by the Chinese in the 1300s. Even your fundamental views of the Old Testament came from the Middle East and the cultures native to that region.

So, I am certainly not saying that "your culture" or "your ancestors" didn't contribute significantly and indelibly to the evolution of mankind. I'm saying that no one civilization does it alone, which makes every culture's contribution significant and of value.

Donald: Ok, I've had enough of this…I've sat and heard you spout you liberal, Antifa nonsense for too long…your versions of history are wrong…your facts are wrong!

Me: But, how can facts, which are objective and quantifiable, be wrong?

Donald: Simple…they are alternative facts.

Me: What do you mean by "alternative"?

Donald: People just make up whatever they want, and because there are some numbers and dates behind it, they want to convince everybody it's true…that doesn't make it true! I can do the same thing…matter of fact, I can do it better than you, than most people…and I have! Your facts are just alternatives, so all that's left is for the people to decide what makes the most sense to them—my facts or yours.

Me: So, if I understand correctly, multiple things can be true at once.

Donald: Correct!

Me: And if someone provides an "alternative" to a fact that you don't like or works against your agenda, you can draw attention to this alternative as a way to not only dismiss his or her assertion, but to more importantly resume control of your narrative.

Donald: Correct!

Me: Interesting…so this must be why this preoccupation of "winning" comes up so frequently for you? It's not really about the money or the fame, it is about the control. History is told by the victor and if you've "won," the only "fact" that is remembered is yours…

Donald: I know what happens if you let the enemies get even an inch… it comes back to bite you in the ass! That's why it's complete domination or nothing. My dad might have won the court proceedings against Eisenhower, but he lost his reputation…he lost his good name. The Bavarian government embarrassed my grandfather…he deserved a hero's welcome; instead, they sent him away like a common immigrant. They tried to ruin his legacy. But, not me, I will never let that happen to the Trump name again…not while I'm still breathing. I won't let them control the narratives or the facts…I won't let them win…I WILL…at all costs.

Me: Interesting…but Donald, many powerful men have been in the position you find yourself in now, but trying to avenge perceived wrongdoings or fulfill the unclaimed glory of a predecessor never works out well. Just look at the Roman Empire. When Augustus tried to restore the Roman Empire to its former scope or to the mythologized glory of Ancient Greece, he ultimately failed to sustain it. When Robert Clive, James Wolfe, and Eyre Coote tried to colonize half of the world's population and territory for the British Empire so Britain could rival the scope of the Roman Empire, they ultimately failed to sustain it. You are the leader of one of the most powerful nations in the world, but if you seek complete and absolute power, you won't be able to sustain it. I think that the Coronavirus pandemic has illustrated how tenuous stability can be…health, economy, life, and, especially, control.

Donald: America will survive the pandemic, don't you worry…we will come back stronger than ever.

Me: But, don't you see the connection, Donald? You're masking again… masking your fear of the pandemic because you know you can't control it. This lack of control triggers your coping mechanism—delusional optimism.

Donald: I'm not delusional! I told you…don't call me crazy!

Me: I'm not calling you, crazy Donald. In fact, I think your reaction is quite normal, given your heritage. Trauma can be passed down by generations, and I believe that your ancestors' constant fear of their own mortality has been passed down to you on a physiological level.

Donald: Don't talk about me or my ancestors like that. They were brave…conquerors, emperors! They were the definition of fearless!

Me:… Do you know who Marcel Ravidat is?

Donald: I think you are running out of irrelevant names to bring up, so now you are just making them up.

Me: Haha…he was a mechanic living in the southwest of France who, in 1940, when he was eighteen years old, he accidentally discovered the cave paintings at Lascaux.

Donald: Okkaayyyyy...

Me: These paintings dated back to almost seventeen thousand years ago, which means that the people who drew these paintings probably spent a lot of time in these caves. I don't know if you have ever spent a lot of time in a cave or on a mountain, but it is a very difficult life. Caves are cold and damp and mountains are rocky, dangerous, and notoriously infertile.

Donald: Okayyyy...

Me: What this implies is the inhabitants of this land—your ancestors, most likely—were constantly in survival mode. Whether it was from cold weather, or the unforgiving climate, or the limited crop production, or the subsequent fighting that occurred over the limited resources...the day-to-day life for an ancient "European" was extremely traumatic. By the time the Roman Empire fell in the eighth century, Europe had been in a constant merry-go-round of famine, disease, and war for almost a thousand years.

Donald: You call *me* an exaggerator...

Me: Oh, this is not embellishment. The Black Death wiped out 50 to 60 percent of the European population in the span of twelve years...that's around fifty million people! It is the most catastrophic pandemic in history. Then, to make matters worse, around the same time, from roughly 1337 to 1453, the Hundred Years War fought between the French and the English created so much instability in food and resources that it took both countries hundreds of years—really, until the colonization of the Americas and Asia—for each country to recover economically. If war and plague weren't enough, in 1570, the Little Ice Age commenced. For decades, Europe experienced intense rainfall, falling birth rates, and mass famines. The lower temperatures and the higher costs of living made life so dire that cannibalism became a common occurrence.

Think about your own family. Your mother was born in the middle of World War I and migrated to America as an unofficial indentured servant before she met your father. Your father lost his father when he was twelve years old to an influenza that took millions of people's lives, and he never even got the chance to mourn his dad. Never got the chance to grieve, to be a child, or to develop into an emotionally healthy adult. Consequently, his childhood perversely and incompletely shaped his morality and worldview. Ultimately, you not only internalized his advice…you internalized his trauma. But, while these ways of coping provide psychological bandages in times of crisis, they become infections in times of peace. You have carried the scars of a wound you have not witnessed for so long, you have forgotten what it's like to not be in pain—to feel safe, to be secure, to not feel traumatized.

So, what I'm saying, Donald, is that this constant reminder of the fragility of your existence, the perception of your life's impermanence, and the chronic anxiety accompanied by the persistent lack of access to sustainable resources has created a hereditary trauma. If not managed, this trauma will result in a rampant and uncontrollable impulse to eliminate, neutralize, or dominate anything or any person you feel poses a threat to your mortality or your gene pool's resources. If unchecked, your defense mechanisms will instigate conflict instead of facilitating negotiation. If unaddressed, your trauma will be passed down to the next generation and create a new wave of traumatized individuals who seek power and control to combat a threat that never really existed for them.

Donald: You don't know what you are talking about. You can quote whoever you want or diagnose me however you'd like, but it's all bullshit…the real truth is that there is nothing wrong with me…I'm strong…I'm a winner because…

I..AM…AMERICAAAA…

It doesn't matter what we have to do, who we have to kill, what we have to blow up to win—we will win. When we wanted land, we took it from the Indians…it was our destiny, so we manifested it! When we needed our crops picked, we got people who could do it so we could worry about bigger things. When we wanted to control a country, we took out the president or took out its money. I'm not the American DREAM—I'm the American REALITY…it's everybody else who needs a wake-up call. I'm as real as it gets. They can slander me, write lies about me all they want, but at the end of the day, they reap the benefits of what I sow. They just complain because they want a bigger piece of what I feed them. Or they don't have the balls to go out and take it…like I did. Like my father did, like my forefathers did. I don't care what you say, you are born with it or you aren't. They hate because they ain't me. They don't have the "It" factor! They can't have it and they never will….

Me: You know, Donald, that is a very apt comparison…I can see how you would see yourself in America.

Donald: Thankkk yoouuu! You finally accept that I'm right.

Me: Like America, you have been institutionalized, shielded, and enabled by powerful men your whole life, so much so that you have never really had to learn how to reach your full potential.

Donald: There has been no place like America and there won't be any place like America ever again. Everything we have we took or we created. Period!

Me: As the current standing President, I am sure you are somewhat familiar with the Constitution…

Donald: Duhh…one of the greatest documents ever written…could use some of my updates, but hey! Still a fine piece of parchment.

Me: So, you know that kind of important part about "truth being held self-evident" and "that men are created equal" and are given these "inalienable" rights…ring a bell so far? You know—life, liberty, and the pursuit of happiness? Yeah, Thomas Jefferson took that from John

Locke, an English philosopher. Or the "separation of church and state"... that was Voltaire, a French writer. Or maybe that "government is made of a social contract between the government and the people"? That was Rousseau, a Swiss philosopher. Or, that there should be a "separation of powers" in the government: judicial, legislative, and—your job—executive. From Montesquieu! Who you can guess, by his name, is not American.

All of the major aspects of your politics have been inherited from European thinkers, but it doesn't stop at politics. The American working-class model, innovations in manufacturing, and the capitalist philosophy are the foundations of every aspect of American business and economy. All of these technologies stemmed from the Industrial Revolution—in Britain. All of the ground-breaking scientific discoveries in physics, mathematics, biology, and chemistry that revolutionized American medicine, technology, and militarism came from...central Europe. The humanities, the liberal arts, and fundamental American architectural aesthetics originated from the creativity of the Italians during the Renaissance. The unapologetic desire to conquer, explore, and traverse never-before-seen new worlds and uncharted territories came from the first European explorers—the Spanish and the Portuguese. Even the gods Americans pray to and the churches we build to worship them are heavily influenced by the Protestants—which we can thank Northern European Reformation for. America was designed to "win," not unlike you, Donald. You are an ambitious, privileged man who grew up in a sixteen-room mansion in the world's richest area codes at a time of unprecedented American global influence. You inherited a thriving real estate company that was supplemented with nepotistic political and legal connections. Like America, you have had your accomplishments prescribed to you by interested parties committed to reaping the benefits of your success. The sheltering of said success has continued into your current years as president, only now, you have special interest groups and entire governments to enable you. You, like America, have "won" before you even played the game and your attempts to avoid this reality creates insecurity, and this insecurity causes you to overcompensate.

Donald: There is nothing insecure about me! I'm a winner and no one can take that from me! Everybody respects and loves winners…everybody loves and respects me!

Me: Understood, so at this stage of your life, with things going for you as they are…what does "winning" look like now for you?

Donald: I want people, years from now, to remember me as the man who returned America to its greatness…that a TRUMP made America great again. So, short-term, that starts with a healthy economy, because, before anything else, I'm a businessman, but also, as I get older, I get more concerned with my legacy. I've had money all my life, but I can't take it with me…the legacy, though…the Trump legacy…can last forever.

Me: I truly do believe you. That you love this country, given your relationship to it. In a way, you believe that you ARE this country. You have always felt like the an outsider, a new kid on the block trying to make a name for himself, whether it was young Donald infiltrating the old money real estate of the Upper East Side or the married Donald that kicked in the door of the well-established casino industry, or the reality star Donald that got into television, or the current Donald that is "draining the swamp" of all the corruption on Capitol Hill. I get it… America is a young and up-and-coming country, too. Only two hundred years old but battling thousand-year-old cultures and traditions in the Middle East, India, and, of course, China for global dominance and respect. And, like America, you feel a sense of entitlement over your global status because the majority of your uniqueness has been inherited, not designed. But you have to remember, Donald, a country, not unlike yourself, is more than the capital it generates. The job of a leader is to ensure the mental, spiritual, emotional, and physical well-being of his or her followers.

Donald: Everything is better when you have a strong economy…I mean, money can't buy you happiness, but it can get you pretty close!

Me: That's a fair, debatable point, so are you saying that having a "good economy" and "ensuring your legacy" are equivalent?

Donald: Yup, whatever it takes…at all costs.

Me: But, the problem is that your motives are not congruent with your goal.

Donald: huh?

Me: Right…"English"…it's not advisable for you to "win at all costs," because you place that objective over the collective welfare of your followers.

Donald: I still don't get what you are getting at…spit it out!

Me: Do you know what the Wollman rink, the Golf Courses, the Trump Tower, the Coronavirus, and your marriages all have in common? You made them all about you, and you didn't care about the collateral damage caused as long as you "won at all costs."

When your goal is to not just succeed, to not just "win," but win at all costs, you put everyone and everything else that is not your goal in jeopardy. If you lose everything around you that you need or care about, by the end of your "mission," when the "great scorer" tallies up your points, you will come up short…every time. Because you can't do it alone…you cannot survive, if you are alone.

Donald: The winners will survive.

I will survive

I have to survive

I have to

Tape stops

"Woof! Woof! Sawyer, what are you—hey, kids! hey, hon! It's so good to see you all! How was your day? Did you guys remember your masks? Okay good, good. Hope you missed the rain…it was really coming down earlier. Ohh…let me just move my stuff to the office…sorry, babe…No, no you guys keep the dining room table…I'm on a deadline. My night is just getting started."

■ ■ ■

Alright, break's over...I said I wasn't going to turn on the news and look at me now...

Okay...Ahh, yeah, one of my more intriguing clients...

Presses Play of "Black Lives Matter July 17th Recording"

Me: Good morning, nice to finally meet you!

Black Lives Matter: Nice to meet you, as well! I'm excited to get started...haha...little anxious, too.

Me: Yeah, I apologize. My schedule has been crazy...lots of people needing support during this quarantine.

Black Lives Matter: Oh, yeah, I bet...2020 has been like an—

Me: Apocalypse?

Black Lives Matter: An awakening, I was gonna say...a revolution.

Me: Hmmm...yeah, there has certainly been a lot to process...so what brings you in? Well, actually...I'm silly...I'm getting a bit ahead of myself...we haven't been officially introduced.

Black Lives Matter: Well, most people know me as Black Lives Matter but I'm not really into labels.

Me: May I call you Black for short?

Black: Sure!…Also, my pronouns are they/them/their.

Me: Hmm…kay…sorry, one second, I just want to make sure I'm getting this all down. "they..theeem"…Alright, got it…is there a particular reason you wanted me to highlight that information?

Black: So, we are clear on my boundaries from the jump…I am a spectrum of Blackness, queerness, and gender that can't be defined so, ya know…address but don't categorize.

Me: Understood, I will do my best. Okay…so, in that spirit, would it be fair to "address" you as a movement?

Black: I mean…when I've made moves, I meant them…so I guess…

Me: Got it, alright, soo if you are ready…let's dive in. What brings you in, Black?

Black: Well, when 2020 started…I was soo happy because 2019 was soo trash and my New Year's resolution was to focus on my self-care more, you know? For as long as I can remember, I have just been putting out fires, running into burning buildings, and just showing up for everybody but myself. Don't get me wrong—I love what I do but, sometimes, you know, every once in a while, it's good to check in with yourself, you know…rescue myself, for once, you know?

Me: Of course, of course…mental health is extremely important, not just in times of crisis but to prevent times of crisis…absolutely…

Black: So, I had all intentions, right, of making an appointment but then Corona hit and that just thew all my plans out the window…and that was a lot because I wasn't just busier than I have ever been…I found myself more isolated than I have ever been, as well. All of a sudden, I wasn't just running into folks at protests or rallies or brunches… I mean, I wasn't alone, but I was lonely…you know?

Me: Of course, of course.

Black: And then Breonna Taylor was tragically murdered…which, don't even get me started on, because the Governor of Kentucky is on all sorts of bullshit, but whatever, she was murdered, and then the Ahmaud Arbery video surfaced and I think that, instead of taking time for myself—you know, to focus on me—I just reacted! Like, I sprang into action because it's like second nature to me.

Me: Yeah, in times of extreme change and jarring discomfort, we often retreat to patterns of behavior that feel familiar to us so we can regain a sense of normalcy…sure, I understand.

Black: Right, Right! Like I wanted to just feel like me again. But, anyway, I mean, I have no regrets for showing up for them because, honestly, who else will, you know? But anyway…that was a lot but then George Floyd gets murdered and when I tell you I didn't want to get out of bed for like days…OOOOh…I was so madd…like they really just don't give a fuck about us…like…I can't even.

Me: I understand why you would feel that way…that video was terrifying.

Black: But you know what made it worse…Trump and the rest of his White supremacist folks took his death as an opportunity to attack me! To attack all my people…calling me a symbol of hate…this corny dude who literally disrespects people on the daily is calling me a symbol of hate?! Boy, you must be out your mind! But anyways, that wasn't even the worst part; my own people didn't even have my back!

Me: Well…I certainly don't know all of the particulars around the protests and the activism around George Floyd's passing—

Black: Murder.

Me: Yes, excuse me, his murder, but I recall there being such an overwhelming outpour of support in local marches and city-wide protests across the globe.

Black: Yes, and I'm appreciative of that, I really am, but the way people polarized my message. The way people co-opted the movement to fit their narrative, was just honestly too much, which is kinda why I set up this appointment. I needed some time to sort out how I feel about everything, you know, to get my mind right.

Me: Well, in order to know where you are going, you have to know where you've been…so let's start there.

Black: I mean okayy. Honestly, in like, sci-fi movies, you never see Black people…it's like they don't expect us to live that long so if revisiting the past helps us get to the future…I'm down.

Me: Well, Let's start at the beginning. Where are you from?

Black: So…I was born in 2013–

Me: Really…Wow! You seem so much older…

Black: Yeah, I get that often, so you know who Trayvon Martin was right?

Me: Yes, of course, another tragic death.

Black: Right, so in 2012, George Zimmerman murdered Trayvon in Sanford, Florida, while he was unarmed, walking home from the convenience store, and minding his own business. Even though he had an iced tea and some Skittles and was seventeen…Trayvon was perceived as a threat, just because he was Black and wearing a hoodie. George Zimmerman wasn't even the police! He was just some dude. Anyways, forty-four days…it took forty-four days and a million people to sign a petition for them to arrest Zimmerman…which is insane, because if Trayvon was White…Hmmph! Them folks would have ran up into his house that NIGHTT. But let me take a breath (inhales…exhales) Okay, I'm back…so, anyway, they had a trial because Florida has a "Stand Your Ground" law that allows people to use firepower to defend themselves if they feel threatened, which is ridiculous because George is really a whole grown-ass man and Trayvon was a boy…someone's child…walking in his own neighborhood! So, he went to trial.

Me: If I remember correctly…they—

Black: Yesss, found this dude innocent. The devil was on his shit that day…I tell you. But after they released the verdict, my auntie, Auntie Alicia, tweets "Black people, I love you, I love us. Our lives matter, Black Lives Matter."

Me: Powerful.

Black: Then my other auntie, Auntie Patrisse, turned those last three words—my name—into a hashtag and, so, on March 7, 2013, I went viral…Black Lives Matter was born.

Me: Interesting.

Black: Yeah…I'm a Pisces so, you know, I can be sensitive but if I mess with you—

Me: "Mess" with you?

Black: Haha…like if I feel emotionally secure with you and, honestly, even if I don't fully, I will show up for you all day, everyday…often at the expense of myself.

Me: Oh, I understand.

Black: So, my other auntie, Auntie Opal, offered to take care of me… you know, build social media platforms so I could connect with other activists my age or mentors I could look up to…

Me: It does take a village, but you have a lot of aunts. Did your parents grow up in a big family?

Black: Oh, they're not my real aunties…Auntie Alicia, Alicia Garza, Auntie Patrisse Cullors, and Auntie Opal Tometi are not even related, but they are close to each other, like sisters. They are more like my legal guardians. They are the ones that dropped me off earlier. I never knew my parents…

Me: That must have been hard.

Black: Honestly, I grew up with so much love and solidarity in the household, like my Uncle Frank—

Me: Ohh…Dr. Frank Leon Roberts, right? Hmm, where do I know that name from?

Black: When I was like, really young—like learning to read and just starting school—he made a whole syllabus for me...They teach it in classes in universities!

Me: It sounds like, even though the circumstances around your birth were a bit morose, you seemed to find a lot of love and support in your early years.

Black: So, you remember when I was telling you that people were trying to come for me this year?

Me: Right, I believe you said "co-opting" you.

Black: Right, so that didn't just start...I've been dealing with that for as long as I can remember.

Me: What do you mean?

Black: Well, after I went viral, all of these other names started popping up...like BLUEE Lives Matter, or Black...GUNSS... Matter. ALL Lives Matter.

Me: Well, when a brand or a nickname becomes popular or trendy, it's common for derivations of that name to arise...it's usually a form of flattery.

Black: I wasn't flattered, and it wasn't flattering...it was subversive.

Me: Expand on that for me.

Black: Just because I assert that my life matters, doesn't mean that yours doesn't, so there is no need to substitute "Black" for "Blue"... blue is not even a racial group! There is no historical precedence for the marginalization of "blue" people...you sound dumb. And to have the audacity to replace "life" with a word that takes away life—"guns"—is not only super problematic but also just soo off-base. You are not the Black Panther Party….please take two seats…

Me: What do you mean by that?

Black: The Black Panther Party was a popular Black empowerment movement in the 60s and 70s that had a policy of open carry. They were frustrated with police coming into Black neighborhoods and not protecting or serving, so they exercised their constitutional right to bear arms to protect themselves from trigger-happy police.

Me: Got it…but what does that have to do with Black Guns Matter?

Black: Well, I have a lot of respect for the Black Panther Party, but we've seen this movie before. When you tell someone that arming themselves is all that "matters," then you not only devalue the other tools of liberation…health, wealth, equality, etc., but you also license deadly weapons in neighborhoods that have not properly dealt with their trauma. People who may be in domestic violence situations that threaten their loved ones. Not to mention, easier access for children to not only harm others but harm themselves! I understand protecting yourself, but you have a responsibility to protect others as well and guns are not a suitable alternative survival strategy to "life."

Me: You mentioned one other name…I think it was…

Black: Ughhh…"All Lives Matter." Do you notice that the majority of people who say, "all lives matter," are usually dusty ol' White supremacists? Them or the those that propagate or profit from patriarchy. How can all lives matter if your actions clearly show that Black lives don't matter…You. Sound. Dumb. Plus, my life mattering doesn't detract from your life mattering; you are just trying to antagonize me.

Me: Interesting…well, if appropriation is a persistent problem, why not go more micro with the labeling…describe yourself in a way that zeroes in on the specific issues you are addressing, like "Criminal Justice Reform" or "People against Police Brutality."

Black: Because that's not comprehensive enough…systemic racism and institutionalized discrimination affect every facet of Black life… the justice system is just the tip of the iceberg and Black people are the Titanic…

Me: Yes. But terms like "systemic racism" are not as intuitive as you may think they are.

Black: Seems intuitive enough to me.

Me: Well, and I'm simply playing devil's advocate, what system are you referring to in "systemic racism"? How exactly does racism present itself in the Black community and what is the difference between racism, discrimination, prejudice, and inequality? What's the difference between system and systemic? Racial disparity and racial bias? They are all interconnected, but without being specific about these differences in your messaging, you elicit confusion and confusion can lead to cooption and subversion.

Black: See, this is why Black people are wary of therapists, and why we need more therapists of color. I'm not sure if you are a person of color or not but you certainly don't know enough about the Black experience. Your playing "devil's advocate" is really just you shifting the responsibility towards the victim to heal what the culprits broke…it's not my job to spoon-feed awareness to folks who can't even be accountable for their own toxicity.

You know, you are really on some pseudo-science b.s, huh…that "Freudian" stuff…asking about my childhood…girl bye… spoiler alert!

you can't have an Electra complex if your father wasn't around, soo…try again! I mean, why do I need to relive my trauma so that you can sympathize with me? See me as human. If you were Black, then we would have never had to go through this.

Me: Well, I might not be Black, but I assure you, I have your best interest in mind.

Black: Well, I'm real interested to know what that interest is because it doesn't seem like the "best" to me. There has been a long history of "scientists" trying to do what is best for Black people and nine times out of ten, they've been shady as fuck.

When African women go for "birth control" or for "vaccines," somehow, magically, their uteruses get removed! And that's present day! Don't even get me started historically. "Scientists" used to measure Black people's skulls because they thought the bumps and grooves somehow proved our lack of intelligence, when the only ones who were unintelligent were these scientists! Eugenics, the idea that personality traits and characteristics can be inherited, was the "science" that was used by the Nazis and the White supremacists that came after them to justify eradicating species. Samuel Cartwright…do you know who that is?

Me: I can't say that I do…

Black: Samuel Cartwright was a whole-ass doctor. Got his medical degree from the University of Pennsylvania and was a well-respected clinician. In 1851, he wrote a whole paper about the "diseases and physical peculiarities of the Negro race" to justify slavery. He made up a name for it and everything. He said the desire for slaves to be free from servitude was called Drapetomania and that slaves should be kept in a "submissive" state and treated like children because they didn't have the mental capacity to run their own lives. So when you claim to have my "best interest" at heart in the name of "science," it sounds real suspect to me, especially when, historically, the only people scientists want to help is their goddamn selves.

Me: Hmmm, wow that is certainly a lot to process and I sincerely appreciate your candid and honest feedback. I can't speak for the intentions or shortcomings of scientists and therapists historically or generally, but I do believe that, like me, Psychology is a constantly-evolving field that strives to grow and get better. I have to believe that is the spirit of science, even if it is not always the outcome. I hope in time you can learn to trust that. With that in mind though, I want to be clear. I'm not here to just validate you. I'm here to help and hopefully heal. In order for me to do that, it means that you need to do the work...

So let's make a deal. I promise to keep this space safe, if you promise to get more comfortable being unsafe...Deal?

Black: Okay...bet.

Me: Huhhh...bet?

Black: Oh, my goodness haha, (overly proper) Yes, you have a deal.

Me: Fantastic!

Tape stops

"Gotta stretch...leg is cramping...alright...*exhales*...you got this..."

Presses Play of "Black Lives Matter July 1st Recording"

Me: Hey! I'm glad you decided to come back! I know our last session was a bit tense.

Black: Yeah, it was a lot, I just needed to process what you were saying, but I'm good.

Me: Great, so should we pick up where we left off? I think we were talking about the Zimmerman trial???

Black: Soo, yeah…I really hit the ground running after the trial. Was learning the lay of the land fast in 2014, despite the appropriators. I thought a lot of people were starting to understand how critical my work was—really, OUR work as a country was—but then July happened… messed up my whole summer vibe and everything.

Me: What happened in July?

Black: NYPD officer Daniel Panteleo stole Eric Garner's life because of LOOSE. CIGARETTES. And, tragically, his last words, "I…can't… breathe," ring in my ears and rang the alarm to Black people that America was suffocating us…and it didn't care if we caught our breath or not.

Me: I remember that video…quite horrific.

Black: What's horrific was that this cop didn't lose his job for FIVE YEARS and even worse, the grand jury refused to press charges…and then, when we are still reeling from the murder of Eric Garner, Darren Wilson guns down an unarmed teenager, Mike Brown…like a coward… and—shocker—he isn't charged! So, I hit the streets so that the world knew our pain.

Me: Did they?…Know your pain?

Black: Not enough of them did.

Me: How did that make you feel?

Black: Mad as hell at first…but after a while…just confused…like I really needed to understand why this was still happening to us and, more importantly, what I was going to do about it!

Me: Sure…

Black: So I started to look at the syllabus Uncle Frank wrote for me and that was great: Marc Lamont Hill's *Nobody: Casualties of America's War on the Vulnerable*, Michelle Alexander's *The New Jim Crow: Mass Incarceration in the Age of Color*, and Angela Davis's *Are Prisons Obsolete"*…oh my God…I just love her! But, anyway, I just wanted to know more. I had so many questions, like how long have we been dealing with these injustices…and what have we done in the past?

Me: That's pretty wise of you…history repeats itself so it makes sense to start with the past for guidance.

Black: Yeah, so, I started with the OGs

Me: O…G's???

Black: Ha! Some of the original activists…some of the most influential Black movements.

Me: Interesting…like who?

Black: Well, if we really want to start in the beginning, the Haitian Revolution was like huge…not only did the Haitians gain their independence around the same time as America, but it was the first slave colony in the Western Hemisphere to win its independence…now that's gangsta…you know because of original…gang…never mind—you look so confused right now! Ha, so anyway, this act of rebellion, act of liberation spurred a revolution of thought and so many influential thinkers…

like Abolitionist Martin Delany and Henry McNeal Turner to name a few. Really helped shaped this idea of Black Nationalism.

Me: What's Black Nationalism?

Black: Black Nationalism is this socio-political and economic empowerment movement that encourages Black people to resist assimilation into Whiteness and institutions that uphold oppression. To build a nation by us for us.

Me: So…and I say this sensitively, of course…

Black: Haha, don't be scared…that was like weeks ago…but watch yourself, though.

Me: So why didn't you?

Black: Why didn't we do what?

Me: Build a nation for Black people…I mean, it sounds like you had an encouraging head start at the time…

Black: Because colonialism doesn't take a day off…

Me: What do you mean?

Black: After the French got dismissed, Haitians were out here living their best lives and these sore losers came back with their ships surrounding Port-Au-Prince, threatening to infiltrate and exterminate the Haitians if they didn't pay for "lost" and "damaged" property. Property meaning PEOPLE…so the Haitians had a tough choice to make! Death or debt and they chose debt…90 million francs! A debt valuing more than 21 billion dollars by today's currency! And it took until 1947 for the Haitians to pay just the interest off that debt. It was only after the earthquake in 2010, almost two hundred years later after Haiti declared independence from France, that the French waved this "Independence Fund" from the Haitians. Haiti was one of the richest countries in history at the time…two-thirds of the sugar and tobacco came from Santo Domingo and the French stole those assets from them. Not to mention, the Americans facilitated this looting, especially after Napoleon gave them the Louisiana Purchase…the bank that handled the transfer of funds was National City Bank or, as you may now know it, just Citibank.

Me: Fascinating…

Black: It's not fascinating…it is EVIL and what's more evil is that about six years after this country gets wrecked by an earthquake AND a hurricane that killed at least 100,000 people, the President has the nerve to call this place a "shithole"….like I can't even with that dude…I. CAN.NOT.

Me: I understand that frustration.

Black: So, after witnessing what France did to Haiti, Black nationalists came up with different ideas on how to build self-sufficient Black communities. Among the most influential ideas was "Garveyism."

Me: "Garveyism"…I'm not sure I'm familiar with that.

Black: So, Garveyism is a philosophy inspired by Marcus Garvey, a Jamaican political activist, entrepreneur, publisher, and a whole other bunch of things. He was born sometime in the 1880s, I think, and was the head of the Universal Negro Improvement Association in the 1910s and 1920s. Garveyism was, and maybe still is, one of the most influential Black nationalist movements in history.

Me: What made Garveyism so impactful?

Black: Well, the main premise of Garveyism was to unify and empower all descendants of Africa under one collective banner so that we could repatriate to Africa. I really gravitated to this idea because it reminds Black people that, despite our differences, culturally and geographically, we need to be unified…that's how the colonizers win—when they divide us. But more important than that, Garvey was known for affirming the beauty of Blackness, our hair, our skin…everything that made us unique…and I thought that was really powerful because when we affirm our beauty, it promotes pride in our culture. It promotes higher self-esteem. I took that lesson and applied it in my own way. I try to unify as many of us as possible because it shouldn't matter your gender orientation, sexual preference, or political affiliation; if you are Black, you are beautiful.

Me: So was Marcus Garvey the only Black nationalist you drew inspiration from?

Black: No, not by a long shot. In America, around the same time as Marcus Garvey, late 19th century, early 20th century, Booker T. Washington and W.E.B Dubois (or William Edward Burghardt) were kind of leading rival Black nationalist movements on their own.

Me: What do you mean by "rival"?

Black: Well, Booker T. Washington was born into slavery and grew up in the harsh, segregated, post-Reconstruction South. This is the south that most people think of when they think about racism—old, conservative, ignorant southerners restricting water fountains, bathrooms, restaurant entry, and lynching folks.

Me: Got it.

Black: So, his strategy was geared around business, education, and entrepreneurship as a path towards self-sufficiency. He was one of the founders of the National Negro Business League. He figured that if Black people focused on educating ourselves, building capital and ownership, that eventually White people would appreciate the value of Black communities. They'd want to invest in us, and, consequently, respect our contribution to American society.

Me: Well, that seems reasonable enough.

Black: Well, it was reasonable until the Greenwood Massacre exposed a flaw in Washington's strategy.

Me: Greenwood?

Black: Yeah, in 1921, Greenwood, Oklahoma, affectionally known as Black Wall Street because of its thriving businesses, offices, and schools, was burned down by the local White residents because they were jealous of how much the Black community was thriving in comparison to them. This incident showed that White people are only invested in Black wealth when it generates even more wealth for White people. If Black people prosper independently of White people, White people will react vengefully.

Me: That's a disturbing theory…

Black: So, William Edward Burghardt had another strategy…a "rival" strategy. He was a really famous Black intellectual, got his bachelor's at Fisk University—designated as one of the Historically Black Colleges and Universities, or HBCUs—then became the first Black person to get his Ph. D in Sociology from Harvard University. His idea was that Black people needed swift and focused political action and a civil rights agenda. He later became one of the founders of the NAACP—the National Association for the Advancement of Colored People. He thought that it didn't matter how much capital you generated or money you have if there are political and institutional policies that sustain inequality.

Me: What type of policies?

Black: Lack of access to healthcare, biased conviction rates, lack of public school funding…you name it!

Me: Got ya, so where do you fit into all of this?

Black: Well, I'm clearly heavily inspired by the social justice aspect of W.E.B Du Bois's strategy, but I just try to pick and choose the attributes of these movements I gravitate to and keep it moving, because the more I learned about Booker T. and W.E.B, the more it got a little suspect…

Me: What do you mean, "suspect"?

Black: Well, so you know how I was talking earlier about Marcus Garvey, right?

Me: Yeah…

Black: Well, after a few assassination attempts and his arrest for mail fraud, his businesses weren't doing so well and his support was waning, so Garvey thought he would go seek support from the KKK!
Me: Why would he do that? I thought the Ku Klux Klan is a notorious hate group?

Black: Because he figured that at the end of the day…they both wanted the same thing…for Black people to essentially go back to where they came from.

Me: Did it work?

Black: Of course, it didn't work and after that, people couldn't take him that seriously and neither could I…I'm never going to be down with White supremacy…no sir…you got the wrong one.

Me: Well, there was still Booker T. Washington and W.E.B Du Bois to look for guidance .

Black: Ehhhh…not reallllyyy thooo….like Booker T. Washington was kind of way to into capitalism for me…capitalism is not the answer to Black liberation…I mean, I'm all about self-sufficiency, though! I fully support urban farming.

Me: What's that?

Black: Growing our own food in neighborhoods that are food deserts. Creating ways to give ourselves adequate supplies of nutrition instead of spending money on non-Black-owned restaurants that provide little economic circulation to our communities…like liquor stores and convenience stores.

Me: Got ya.

Black: Yeah, most Black-owned businesses are run by sistas and I love that! So, I'm all for getting your coin, but remember you came to this country as CAPITAL, not a person. So investing in a system that was designed to exploit, doesn't seem like the end-all-be-all to me.

Me: Well, what about W.E.B Du Bois's strategy…

Black: Listen, I'm really not trying to hate on him because he was biracial or whatever…if you have one drop of Black in you…YOU'RE BLACK…trust. I'm not into that colorism nonsense but dude was really trying to say that social change would only be accomplished by developing a small group of college-educated Black elites called the

"Talented Tenth"…umm, excuse me…that does not sound inclusive at all…it sounds mad shady…like I'm sorry but who are you to determine what type of Black is acceptable or not? That supremacist stuff is rooted in patriarchy and I'm not here for it…like I'm sorry, but I'm just NOTTTTT.

Me: Understood, understood.

Black: So yeah, I put the books down and went back to what I do best… action!

Me: And what did that look like?

Black: Well, Obama was still in office at the time, which meant that the President and the Attorney General were both Black and I was going to make sure they didn't forget it.

Me: I remember that. I think the President said something like, "If I had a son, he would look like Trayvon"…

Black: Right, right all that, and you know we were making some progress, baby steps, like he established consent decrees.

Me: Consent decrees?

Black: Consent decrees allowed overhaul of police departments charged with civil rights violations.

Mes: Got it.

Black: Yeah, he limited the amount of military grade weapons the police had access to and set up investigations for police departments that show a pattern of discriminatory behavior or abuses of power.

Me: That sounds substantial…

Black: Like I said, it was a step in the right direction, but all that changed when the Cheeto-in-Chief got elected…

Me: You are talking about President Donald J. Trump?

Black: I mean, that might be your president, but that's not MY president.

Me: Interesting.

Black: Dammnn…why is everything so interesting to you?? Like it's really not…it's CRAZY!

Me: It's just how I process information…I won't say it anymore if it makes you uncom-

Black: Don't even worry about it haha…you do you.

Me: So, how did the election of "my" president affect you?

Black: Well, for one, it reaffirmed that I need to get more organized and kind of solidify my structure.

Me: How so?

Black: Well I have been advocating for defunding the police since 2016, so that didn't really change. I really wanted to show financial support for families of those murdered by the police. But, even outside of criminal justice reform, I have been advocating for education reform, access to better healthcare, and more mental health support for Black people for a minute, but there are so many different issues that Black people face, it's impossible for one person to do everything. So, by that time, we had created thirteen official chapters in the U.S and three more in Canada.

That way, each chapter can do the work that makes sense for its local community. The chapters are semi-autonomous, so they can work nationally and locally at their discretion.

Me: What do you mean by "semi-autonomous"?

Black: Like the Chicago chapter focuses a lot on police accountability, but the Boston chapter does a lot or work around mutual aid... every chapter addresses what is most urgent locally and, sometimes, nationally and in 2017, I became global...the Black Lives Matter Global Network Foundation, Inc.

Me: Wow, that's quite a journey from a hashtag...but why decide to go global? I thought you were focused on Black issues locally in the United States?

Black: Because of Atatiana Jefferson, Willie McCoy, Botham Jean.

Me: Who are they?

Black: Exactly, they are the ones that got murdered unjustly and that nobody knows about—that didn't get the media attention because they weren't cisgendered, heterosexual African American men. The homeless, the immigrants, or the refugees are, for some reason, not worth our outrage...but they were worth mine...because they were Black and their lives mattered.

Me: How were you affected by these murders?

Black: I'm not going to lie...it fucked me up. You remember the Charlottesville riots...you know, when a bunch of White supremacists attacked protesters petitioning to remove the confederate statue in Virginia?

Me: Yes, I do remember.

Black: And do you remember what Trump said when one of the White supremacists ran over protesters with his car???

Me: Umm…I think he said—

Black: That there were good people on both sides! What?!? Are you kidding me? That's when I knew things were going to get worse before they got better. I mean, if he doesn't even care about the lives of Americans, how could he care about the lives of the un-documented? Or the refugees seeking political asylum? Let me answer that for you…he won't! And so I said to myself, someone has to…

Me: So what did you do?

Black: Well, Auntie Opal gave me some books to read and some documentaries to watch and I went to work.

Tape stops

"Alright..fast forward..okay, here we go…"

Presses Play of "Black Lives Matter July 15th Recording"

Me: So, last time, you said you went to "work"—what did you mean by that?

Black: I wanted to know how I could show up for ALL Black people and I wanted to know how others have done so in the past.

Me: Intere…uhhh…ha. So, what did you find out?

Black: So, you know how I mentioned W.E B Du Bois before?

Me: Yes.

Black: Well, I'm not sure if you've ever read the *Souls of Black Folk*? It's like one of his most famous books, but, in there, he describes how colonization created a "double consciousness" for Black people…

Me: Hmmm, I'm sort of familiar with this term…but please elaborate more.

Black: He essentially described how Black people have to live between two identities in America. They can live their true authentic Black self when they are at home and in their community, but have to suppress their Blackness when they enter or assimilate into White communities, which leads to a sort of "double-consciousness," a split between two worlds.

Me: Fascinating…

Black: Right, well this brotha, Frantz Fanon, kind of took it to another level. He argues that since the 1600s, every pan-African country, colony, or community that has been colonized by some type of European colonial power has been subjugated or destroyed by this sort of double-consciousness because colonization destroys everything native to your culture and replaces it with everything native to the oppressor's culture…which, in turn, makes you hate Blackness and idolize Whiteness.

Me: So, why were you particularly drawn to…what did you say his name was again?? Frann..

Black: Frantz Fanon…I mean "drawn" is kind of strong…I wouldn't say all that, like he is from Martinique, but he wrote his first book in France, *Black Skin White Mask,* and I swear it should have been called Black Skin…White Mas-Cara all over my….you know what…I am not even going to read him today, even though he sure did love those White women, sheesh!…Love is love….love…isss…love…okay, I'm back, I'm back.

Me: (Chuckles)…good, good, so you were saying? You felt connected to him because…?

Black: Because Fanon kind of reminds me that the Black struggle in Uganda, or Botswana, or the Bahamas, or Bahia is all rooted in the same psychological struggle for decolonization. Steve Biko was profoundly influenced by Frantz Fanon.

Me: Steve Biko…

Black: Everybody knows of Nelson Mandela and his push for peace and truth and reconciliation, which—don't get me wrong—is amazing. I hold folks accountable all the time…should call it truth and reparations, but I digress…Steve Biko helped create the South African Students' Organization in 1968 and he said that the only way to end apartheid is for Black people to empower themselves mentally. You have to remember that Black people are the majority in South African, but the minority, the Dutch, owned most of the land and the assets. How? Because they kept up the illusion that they deserved it. That stability comes when the wealthy, racial elite have all the power. He fought for folks to speak truth to that power…and it cost him his life.

Me: I understand.

Black: See, whether your oppressor was the British, or the French, or the Dutch, or the Germans, or whomever…Black people have to collectively reclaim our culture…reclaim our Blackness. So there is a lot that can be learned or applied in America from our brothers and sisters on the continent and in the Caribbean.

Me: Can you expound on that?

Black: So the nineteen fifties, sixties, and seventies were a really revolutionary time. Not just for America, but for countries abroad. Like, in 1957, Ghana finally declared independence from Britain and, in 1960, it approved a new constitution and elected Kwame Nkrumah as the president.

Me: Respectfully…why was this so momentous?

Black: Because it was one of the first times since the Haitian Revolution where Black people saw a Black country gain its independence that had a political philosophy not rooted in colonialism.

Me: So, you are saying because Ghana wasn't modeled on European or American politics, it could form its own identity?

Black: Yes, exactly! One where it wasn't just solely centered on capitalism but on the good of the people. But, I think of all my favorite African liberators, mine would have to be…Thomas Sankara.

Me: Who is Thomas Sankara?

Black: Who is…what—are you serious? He is the former president of Burkina Faso and he was…IS…a legend. Not only did he domestically focus on agrarian self-sufficiency and land reform to help prevent famines, he also prioritized education with a nationwide literacy program; promoted public health by vaccinating 2.5 million children against meningitis, yellow fever, and measles; planted more than ten million trees to combat the desertification of the Sahel; and established a road and railway construction program—all before he died at the age of thirty-seven. That's not even why I rock with him, though. He really got my respect when he outlawed female genital mutilation, forced marriages, and polygamy. He appointed women to high governmental positions and encouraged them to work and stay in school, even if they were pregnant. He was just a rock star and his policies helped remind me that it was okay to want a government that keeps the people—not just the wealthy, but everybody's—best interest at heart.

Me: So, did these "pan-African" liberation movements give you the boost you need?

Black: Well, they did, until it happened again…and again…and again…

Me: Again??

Black: They LYNCHED us publicly…again…Freddie Grey, Tamir Rice, Alton Sterling, Walter Scott, Sandra Bland, Philando Castille…on and on until there are too many to count. I was painfully reminded that the first step in fixing your community, is to fix your household first.

Me: After our last session, I went onto your website and saw that you and other Black civil rights organizations work closely with "A Vision for Black Lives." Was that a sort of response to the policies you want changed in your "household"?

Black: I mean…yeah, like I said, we don't have an agenda in the formal sense…just policies that we support and don't support. So, yeah, an "end to capital punishment" and an "immediate end to the criminalization and dehumanization of Black youth," an "end to mass surveillance of Black communities," and the "demilitarization of law enforcement." A lot of these changes are not new, *per se*. There has been a long legacy of American freedom fighters advocating for these changes.

Me: What do you mean by "legacy"?

Black: Well, remember how I mentioned the Black Panther Movement?

Me: Yes, certainly.

Black: Well, a lot of the policy changes from "A Vision for Black Lives" is inspired by the "ten-point program."

Me: Ten-point program?

Black: Conservatives and Fox News want to make it seem as if Beyonce was some type of "radical" because she put up a Black power fist at the Super Bowl, but people don't do their research! Huey P, Bobby Seale, Elderidge Cleaver…they had their disagreements and they damn sure weren't perfect but, at some point…I would like to say at their best…they wanted prosperity for Black people. They created a free breakfast plan for children and helped set up clinics. Equality was like…in their bible. Decent housing, full employment, free health care, land, bread, housing, education, clothing, justice….peace, you know? The basic things everybody wants, but for some reason, treating Black people like citizens is controversial for some folks.

Me: I would hope not.

Black: Honestly, I really don't know any more…like, I really don't. And, of course, I've taken a lot from the king himself, Martin Luther King, Jr., but I honestly kind of rock with his protege a bit more.

Me: Protege?

Black: Well, yeah that's vague, haha, he had a lot, but I'm talking about the guy he appointed to lead the Student Nonviolent Coordinating Committee: Kwame Ture. Or, as most people know him—Stokely Carmichael.

Me: And why do you identify more with Mr. Carmichael?

Black: Because he was the developer of the Black Power movement!

Me: Black Power…I thought you were more focused on Black empowerment and Black equity?

Black: I am, for sure! Trust that that hasn't changed, but after so many murders and so much protesting, it's clear that if you want to change the system, you are going to have to disrupt the system. Change can't come if people are comfortable. Change can only happen if we are united… if we lean into our power. Did you know that the Black community contributes trillions of dollar to the GDP every year? There is power in our dollar and we are not using it to build ourselves up. That's why it's important to divest from places that don't value us, like the police departments or our local politicians. Melina Abdullah, the co-founder of my Los Angeles Chapter, has been really doing a great job with that.

Me: I think I saw her on CNN…

Black: Probably, probably but…uhh, yeah…I was on my Malcom X stuff: liberation by any means necessary! Militant, vigilant, because in the Trump era you have to be. You know? You can't slip with these people because if they catch you down, they will walk all over you.

Me: Sure, sure…so what changed?

Black: Changed?

Me: Well, as grateful as I am to see you in my office, I am curious about how you got from "vigilance" to "vulnerable."

Black: Hmmm…okay, I see you with your alliteration and shitt… haha…you think you cute, huh? But, anyway, let me stop playing. So, like I was telling you earlier after watching that evil man stand on George's neck for nine minutes, everything just went south.

Me: How do you mean? If I recall, there was a deluge of social and financial support? Am I off base with my recollection?

Black: It's more like you are hitting a foul ball.

Me: Sorry, I don't—

Black: Bases…foul ball…baseball…you know what, let me tone down the sass. So what people don't know is that in the last seven years, I've raised about one hundred thousand in donations and that covers the basic operations of everything. And even though I might have allies with deep pockets…my coins was not busting out the bank. But after the George Floyd protests, we received an overwhelming amount of donations. This caused a lot of confusion around how we would best use the funds. How to be transparent, and how to make sure it went to the right places.

Me: What do you mean the "right places"?

Black: Well, for example, a lot of people would donate to the Black Lives Matter Foundation, which is in no way affiliated with me. The Black Lives Matter Foundation actually wants to bring the community and police together; I want to defund the police and hold the murderers accountable.

Me: I understand.

Black: But that's what I was talking about earlier—co-option has real consequences.

Me: What do you mean?

Black: Like people on the news would COMMEE. FOOR. MEE. Constantly talking out the side of their neck about how I'm only protesting when cops kill Black people, not when Black people kill Black people. Or how the protests lead to riots and looting. Or how the signs at rallies call for violence. But people don't understand; I'm not responsible for how allies choose to show up for me. I am not TELLING or PROMOTING violence in any form. I show up for my people even when the cameras stop rolling and CNN leaves my cities for a sexier story. I can't control what issues people choose to ignore or pay attention to but, somehow…huh…trust that somehow, I get blamed for it and you want to know the most hurtful part? When it comes from your own people.

Me: Can you expound on that?

Black: Okay, well don't get me wrong, there are a lot of folks showing up for me and I do sincerely appreciate them…shout out to City Councilman Herb Wesson Jr. and Council President Nury Martinez in L.A. for approving measures to develop an unarmed model of crisis response that would replace police officers with community-based responders…like, that meant so much.

Me: That sounds encouraging.

Black: Yes, but you have Uncle Toms like Jessie Lee Patterson saying that I am "evil"…and other Black conservatives like Arizona Rep. Walt Blackman calling me a "terrorist organization"…really??? We really going to take it there? I mean, I'm all for civil discourse but there is nothing "civil" about the "course" they are taking…but I do get the "dis" part…

Me: Hmmhmmm.

Black: Like, if you want to be petty, I can get petty…like how you named "Black Man" but you all up in the White Man's—you know what, let me stop….I'm not even gonna go there…wheeeww, when they go low….Lord Jesus…when they go to the basement…take the escalator, girlll…go to the second floorrr.

Me: Hmmm, why do you feel like you are the target of such controversy? Of such contention?

Black: I think it's because I'm young. Black youth have always been viewed as more mature than we are, so they treat us like grown adults.

Me: How so?

Black: Well there has been a long history of folks taking advantage of the innocence of Black children. Black children, especially Black girls, are more likely to get kidnapped, prostituted, sold into sex slavery, or be sexually and physically abused, unfortunately, often in our own communities. But, outside of our communities, doctors will often misdiagnose learning disorders like ADHD or Dyslexia as insolence or disrespect and even prescribe lower amounts of pain medication when Black folks are ill, because they think we have a higher pain threshold than we do. Not to mention how early young Black girls get sexualized as grown women and young Black men get sentenced like grown men. So when I see CNN, NBC, FOX News, or any other media outlet tell my story for me…all I see them doing is sensationalizing Black trauma. They make a spectacle of our deaths and they wonder why we grow up so fast, because Black children have to…I had to.

Me: You have certainly witnessed a lot more death than anybody your age should have to. Developmentally speaking, the side effects are chronic.

Black: That's why I had to take a step back, you know? Make sure I was straight and, honestly, no disrespect to you, but counseling was not my first choice.

Me: What was your first choice?

Black: Spirituality…I just wanted a collective experience, you know? Somewhere where I could be with my people. But again…no shade.

Me: Haha…none taken. So, did you find what you were looking for?

Black: Not quite. So, you remember how I was telling you how I was on my Malcom X stuff?

Me: By any means necessary, right?

Black: Look at you taking notes!! High five! (slapping noise). Okay…so Malcom got me curious about the Nation of Islam, Minister Farrakhan, Allah, the Quran, all of that. And while I have all the respect in the world for my Muslim brothers and sisters, I am not down for some of their conservative views on women's rights. Hmmm hmm…no, not me. No, thank you! That's why I couldn't rock with the Hoteps either.

Me: Hoteps?

Black: The Black Israelites or Black Hebrews…I don't know what they call themselves but I know it's homophobic, transphobic, patriarchal… Uhh, I'm good thanks…Imma just go back to what I was doing before, you know, ensuring prosperity for ALL Black people, not just the cis-gendered hetero ones.

Me: So, is that what you did? Go "back to what you were doing before?"

Black: Well, I figured I would take a look at the religions that were not so Euro-centric…You know…no White Jesus, Greek morals, all that. So I went to the Caribbean…do you know what Santeria is?

Me: I'm familiar with it, but not the intricacies…

Black: That makes sense. Caribbeans call it many names...Regla de Ocha, Regla Lucumi, or just Lucumi. It's popular in the diaspora but was developed in Cuba a couple hundred years ago. It's like a mix of the Yoruba religion and Catholicism, because there are Orishas, which are deities or, like, spirits and Roman Catholic saints. So I liked it because Rastafarianism—

Me: Like in Jamaica?

Black: Yes, exactly! In both religions, Santeria and Rastafarianism, there is no central leadership, which makes it more immune to corruption, because you know, absolute power...

Me: Corrupts absolutely...sure.

Black: Okay, Wikipedia! I see you!!! Anyway, like Santeria, Rastafarianism is also a mix of diasporic African beliefs mixed with Christian ideology, but, unlike Santeria, Rastas are not polytheistic. They believe in one God—Jah.

Me: So, why didn't you gravitate toward Santeria or Rastafarianism? They seem to have a blend of diasporic African traditions and customs that you could potentially identify with.

Black: Because, unfortunately, like many religions, even when there is no central leadership, the masculine energy dominates the space and, honestly, that was pretty discouraging for me.

Me: You know, that's interesting that you say that, because all of the movements you were inspired by seem to be heavily influenced by a strong male presence...where do you think this kind of love/hate relationship with masculinity comes from? Could it perhaps have something to do with the absence of a father figure in your own life? Could you be trying to fill this void of a paternal figure with strong male-lead movements?

Black: See, that's the thing. They really weren't.

Me: Weren't what?

Black: Led by men…cisgendered, heterosexual ones are just the ones that got the credit….that got remembered. Honestly, my aunties reminded me of something I had forgotten: that the hidden figures—shout out to Taraji!—are the real heroes. The ones in the background that change the world in the shadows without ever get bathed in the warmth of praise and adoration…they give me strength:

You don't have an abolition movement without Miss Harriet Tubman and Miss Sojourner Truth. You don't have the NAACP without Ida B. Wells, Ella Baker, Daisy Bates, Septima Clark, and Rosa Parks. Mary McLeod Bethune stared a whole-ass UNIVERSITY…Bethune-Cookman…plus she founded the National Council of Negro Women. Shirley Chisholm was the first Black woman to be elected to Congress.

There are no "divas" without Josephine Baker, no soul without Anita, no rhythm and blues without Aretha, Diana, Gladys…Whitney! You don't have civil rights without Fannie Lou Hammer, Maude Ballou, Claudette Colvin, Mamie Till Mobley, Rev. Dr. Pauli Murray…the list goes on, but please, please don't let me forget about my LGBTQIA+ folks…Phil Wilson, who founded the Black AIDS institute, Barbara Smith, Ruth Ellis, Alice Walker…James Baldwin!!! Not to mention how the Stonewall Riots in 1969, the same uprising that led to decades of human rights legislation and civil rights policy changes, were started by trans folks.

But, you've never heard of them…but they matter…their contributions mattered…their lives mattered, and when we try to exclude the most marginalized, we lose the war before we even start the battle…

Me: Wow, that is certainly…informative.

Black: Well, you're welcome….the more you know…but, that's how they win…when they divide and erase us.

Me: Erase? What do you mean by that?

Black: You remember when I was talking about the Rastafari?

Me: Yes, of course.

Black: Well, obviously, one of the most famous Rastafarians is Bob Marley, right? "One Love"…"No Woman, No Cry"…you know who he is…everybody does. But how do they remember him? For his activism? For his revolutionary music? For his Black nationalism? Nope—they remember him for smoking weed. And, to top it all off, they criminalize Black people for selling weed and then, a few years later, they legalize it and then build all-White corporations around distribution and manufacturing! And why do you think that is?

Me: I'm going to assume that question is rhetorical….

Black: Because White-owned corporations and music labels make more money criminalizing Black people instead of uplifting them. They think it appropriate to appropriate our style, our rhythm, our lyrics, our hair, our bodies, our pain for their profit. Why do you think David Bowie, Boy George, Queen, Motley Crue, the Sex Pistols, and Guns N' Roses all look like they are auditioning for Ru Paul's Drag Race? Because they are all influenced by Little Richard!

There is no Elvis Presley, Rolling Stones, Beatles, Led Zeppelin, Pink Floyd, the Eagles—any of those rock legends you love—without Chuck Berry, Muddy Waters, Bo Diddley, James Brown!

That's why I love music and art, especially as a vehicle of self-expression and healing. But artistic expression causes me anxiety because you can take the style, the look, the culture, and forget the names. In a sense, that anxiety is worse than the police brutality and the incarceration rates because it isn't just the death of our bodies, it's the death of our existence. Our stories…our legacy.

Me: Is your legacy something you think about a lot? How you'll be remembered?

Black: It's not about me. Without legacy, there is nothing for the next generation to hold on to, to live up to. All you have is another generation of children growing up without guidance, which generates more trauma, which dissolves more Black families, and the cycle continues.

Black culture is the most copied, the most appropriated culture in the world, and when White people try to capitalize off it, it feels like they are trying to own us again, like they are trying to attack us, wipe us out. It feels malicious. It feels personal. Like they are threatened by our very existence. But that's why I'm named what I'm named…to remind every Black person that they cannot be erased, that they matter…that Black Lives Matter.

Me: That is certainly a lot to take in, wow…let's put a pin on that thought. But as we pack up here, I want you to know that I respect and receive everything you have just said and I am glad that you feel comfortable enough with me to be vulnerable, but I want you to consider something…I want to challenge you.

Tape stops

"I'm going to need some coffee for this next part. Honey! Can you get me som—Ohh, thank you. I was just calling you…I'll be in bed soon, love. Ahhh…that's good coffee…*Fast forwards*…okay."

Presses Play of "Black Lives Matter July 29th Recording"

Me: So, last session, I talked about how I wanted you to consider something...Are you ready?

Black: I mean, it depends on what you are about to say. I mean, I could be ready to go off or ready to go home...it's honestly up to you, sis.

Me: Have you considered that this sensation you feel, this "threat to the existence of the collective Black culture," is more of a perception than a sensation?

Black: Woooooowwwwww, so, you are saying that I'm imagining the suffering of Black people? That I just made the whole thing up? For what??? You think Black people just like being the victim for no reason?

Me: No, no, of course not. I'm not suggesting that at all. Please don't misunderstand me. I'm simply saying that sometimes the intent of an action can be disparate from the impact of it. For example, my intent is to challenge you, but it seems like my impact has been confrontation... but, just because that was the impact, that doesn't mean my intent can be ignored.

Black: So, let me get this straight...you cause me harm...and I'm supposed to just think about what you meant to say?? Like, NO uhh, uhh... like, who does that?

Me: No, what I'm simply saying is th—

Black: You are simple, yes...very simple, because you are on some basic shit. Black people do not need to think about what you meant. Or what you intended...hmm hmmm...we past all that. When you repeat the same oppression over and over again, you gets no understanding. You gets no "positive intent." Fuck that! You know what? Since you want to ask me all types of triggering questions…fuckin' up my day and shit… let me ask you some questions…see how you like it!

Me: I am open to that…it seems only fair, given the circumstances, and if it will help you gain my trust again, I am more than willing.

Black: So, please tell me EXPPERTTT….Did I imagine the Mississippi Black Codes? Did I imagine Jim Crow?

Me: I am sure you didn't, but please elaborate…

Black: The Mississippi Black Codes were these set of LAWS…and I emphasize LAWS….because this wasn't just a practice, it was legal… like, okayyyedd by the United States government and everything. But anyway, the Black Codes were a set of laws passed first by Mississippi and then, shortly after, by South Carolina, Alabama, Louisiana, Florida, Virginia, Georgia, North Carolina, Texas, Tennessee, and Arkansas as a response to losing the Civil War in 1865. These "codes" authorized harsher sentences, restricted farmland ownership, and, if Black people didn't show proof of occupation when prompted by the police, the punishment was arrest and a fine and that was just the prequel…don't even get me started with Jim Crow! Jim Crow solidified the inequality that the Black Codes started. These laws separated and underfunded public facilities, interstate trains, buses, schools, and hospitals. Jim Crow effectively destroyed any chance that we had at economically, educationally, or socially building generational wealth or opportunity.

But the climax, the finale, the nail in our metaphorical and literal coffins, came when they created the police, because the only reason the police was ever created was to be slave catchers. And why did they want to catch us? Because written in the Thirteenth Amendment, there is a little clause that effectively undoes the emancipation proclamation altogether…and do you know what that clause is?

That if you become a prisoner...the American government has the right to turn you into a slave...so please...tell me...did I imagine that injustice? Are they just "in my head"?

Me: I understand how generational trauma can be passed down, but these practices were over a hundred yea-

Black: Ohhh...so you want the remix? The updated volume? The reboot of racism? Okay...how recently did the CIA insert drugs and guns into urban cities and communities of color? How long ago was the Tuskegee syphilis experiment, where epidemiologists knowingly infected hundreds of Black people without them knowing? How long ago did they deny 1.2 million Black military veterans housing after they fought in World War II? How long ago was it they suppressed the Black vote with underfunded voter booths? Or deny us housing loans? Or bury us with high interest rates for business loans...or effectively devalue the dollars generated by Black homes with redlining?

Am I still playing victim?

America was economically, socially, and philosophically built off of RACISM...not just slavery, but full-blown, well-documented, and malignantly-intentioned bigotry...do you know who Posidonius is? Any American philosopher would probably label him one of the greatest mathematicians and philosophers of all time. He once said that, "those races nearest to the Southern half of the axis do not have enough blood to make them sufficiently human." Hippocrates, as in the Hippocratic oath that doctors take to swear to "do no harm," once said that "dark people were cowards and light people were courageous fighters"...I guess that is where the term hypocritical came from, too, huh?

But since you like recent history, let me give you some. Carl Linnaeus, the founder of modern-day taxonomy, outlined a list of five "varieties of humanity," and I'll let you guess where Black people landed! Immanuel Kant, one of the most influential philosophers on ethics and morality in the last five hundred years, said that stereotypes about other races weren't good or bad but based on "reasoned" philosophy. His eighteenth century fellow French Enlightenment thinker, Voltaire, believed wholeheartedly that different races of people develop differently from each other…I guess we know now what the "lighten" in "Enlightenment" means. But, of course…of course, the Americans had to take the prejudice prize because "we are number one in everything," right? Not only did the founding fathers own slaves, but one of them, Benjamin Rush, went so far as to say that being non-White was a "disease"!

Sooo, are you telling me that I should focus on their "intent"? Focus on what they "meant" to say? Fuck that! You are not going to sit there and tell me to think about the oppressor's feelings. The only feelings I'm concerned with are my peoples'…I am committed to US.

I am committed to embodying and practicing justice, liberation, and peace.

I am committed to practicing empathy, love, and compassion.

I am committed to collectively, lovingly, and courageously working vigorously for freedom and justice for Black people and, by extension, all people.

So when I say it feels personal, deep-rooted, it's not just in my head… it's real! That's the meaning behind my name. It is an act of rebellion against attempts to erase our existence. Like my Auntie Opal says, it is "a call to action, a tool to reimagine, a tool where people are free to exist."

Me: I want to take a moment to just say thank you…thank you for your honesty, earnestness, and candor. I receive it with a full heart and an open mind. It's a lot to process, but please understand me when I say that

I, by no means, mean to diminish the historic injustices and oppression that Black people have faced. I do want you to try something though…

Black: Bu—

Me: Before you say anything, just indulge me. Step outside of yourself, your experience…out of your culture…breathe in…breathe out…and try to look at it from the outside looking in. I know it's difficult, but just try…

Black: (Exhales)…Woo-sah…haha…now what?

Me: Why do you think hip-hop has been so successful?

Black: Excuse me?

Me: Hip-hop—you know…rapping, breakdancing, marketing, designing. It has influenced popular culture for almost forty years…why do you think that is?

Black: Misogyny, homophobia, the commodification of violence…I don't know, commercialized toxic masculinity?

Me: Branding!…They are successful because of branding.

Black: What are you talking about?

Me: Don't get me wrong, you are absolutely correct. It is an absolutely valid critique, but while homophobia and misogyny are integral aspects of the art form, I am not certain that these aspects are what make the art form successful.

Black: And, I would argue that it DOES make hip-hop successful. America—honestly, the world—has had a long track record of glorifying violence and sex in order to bottle it up for consumption, i.e., every blockbuster action movie, every fashion show, every action/adventure video game, every popular music video since the fifties. I mean, it's practically the formula for artistic/commercial success. Hip-hop is just the latest iteration of that cycle.

Me: Certainly! But if what you said was true—if the basis for your premise concerning America's antagonism of Black people is correct—why would an industry, a culture, and a movement be relatively impervious to America's disdain of Blackness?

Black: I don't know…because everybody needs a villain?

Me: Perhaps, but I think, even more fundamentally than that, on a psychological level, we feel we understand hip-hop, we identify with it, and thus, on some primitive level, connect with it.

Black: What do you mean by "connect with it"?

Me: Well, certainly music is a universal language, which is why rap music has persisted longer than the other seminal aspects of the hip-hop movement. But think of how a rap artist brands his or herself…

Black: I'm sorry, but the fact that you keep using Black "branding" in a positive way is kinda funny to me since, historically, slave owners used "brands" to label people as property and now, almost two hundred years later, companies use "brands" to label self-expression as property. We are not always in control of our publishing rights…we don't always control our brands.

Me: Yes, but you control your name!…the lyrics you write!…the melodies you make!…the stories you tell! This, above everything else, is what captures the heart of a fan! Think about it…a rapper usually writes stories of struggle, trauma, and the eventual ultimate triumph over that trauma. Rappers don't work, they "hustle." They don't accomplish, they "shine." They don't simply achieve, they overcome. These messages are universally inspiring. They are universally relatable and significantly contribute to hip hop's transcendence.

Black: Okay…I will concede that White people admire Black strength and resilience but what does that have to do with me?

Me: It has everything to do with you! Or, I should say, in a manner of speaking, it has everything to do with your culture.

Black: What do you mean?

Me: Are you familiar with the concept of Nommo?

Black: I can't say that I am…

Me: The Dogon people of Mali believed that Nommo carries the vital life force, or "Ntu," that produces all life and shapes reality. The Dogon believe that the spoken word is the carrier of this reality-shaping life force.

Nommo is described as a unity of spiritual-physical fluidity that gives life to everything, penetrating everything and causing everything. Since people are the only species that can speak words, they have the most control over this power. When someone speaks or initiates a conversation, he or she directs and shares this life force with the listener This facilitates a personal and collective harmony or "Maat," as known in Ancient Kemetic civilizations, with the speaker and the audience.

Black: Woah, I didn't know that…

Me: We see this same sanctification of the spoken word in the Bible. In the book of Genesis, God said, "Let there be light" and, allegedly, the universe was created. Did you know that the Dogon thought the spoken word was so powerful, they wouldn't name their children at birth? They waited until children were about four or five because they believed that once you name a child, they had muntu.

Black: Muntu?

Me: Yes, muntu is the life force of Nommo combined with an individual's spiritual force that makes the physical body human. The Dogon believed that you couldn't be a physically and spiritually whole person until you had a name. Cognitively speaking, this belief system holds a lot of merit.

Black: How?

Me: Well, in Cognitive Psychology, there is a theory called Spreading Activation.

Black: What's that?

Me: Spreading Activation is the theory of how the brain's memory center organizes itself through a network of associated ideas to retrieve specific information. This information is arranged as cognitive units, each consisting of nodes. Associated elements or characteristics of a specific concept or memory are all connected by habituated neural connections.

Black: Wait, slow down…you are getting a little too heady for me.

Me: Essentially, this theory describes how people organize the understanding of the world with their personal experiences…

Black: Ohh…well, yeah, that's like implicit bias…why didn't you just say that?

Me: It's actually a bit different from implicit bias. Implicit bias refers to the attitudes or stereotypes that affect our understanding, actions, and decisions in an unconscious manner. Spreading Activation is not necessarily based off of attitudes or stereotypes. It is much more cognitively elemental than implicit bias because it is based off an individual's personal experience. Let me give you an example. Let's say you were…I don't know…a Green person and you grew up your whole life around other Green people. Now, you have certainly seen people of other colors: Red, Yellow, etc. Perhaps on TV or as tourists in your primarily "Green village," but you don't have much personal experience interacting with anybody who wasn't Green. Then one day, you encounter a "Purple" homeless person outside of your office building as you leave your job and he asks you for spare change. You politely refuse, but every other day for about six months the Purple beggar stands outside your office at five o'clock faithfully, asking you and your Green coworkers for change. One day, you decide to take a vacation and while you are boarding the plane, a Blue passenger with skin of a rich hue sits next to you and asks if he can switch seats with you. At that moment, irrespective of any stereotypes or preconceived notions you have of Blue people, the visual cue of dark Blue skin is perceptually similar enough to Purple skin that it could urge the Green person to reject the Blue passenger's request without consciously knowing why. The Green person has rejected the request to change seats because his memory has conditioned him to reject skin associated with Purple. Until they have new experiences to void this association, they may unwittingly develop an aversion to "Blue requests," even if they have no specific bias towards Blue people.

Black: Haha, Is this example your subtle way of tricking me into saying "Blue" Lives Matter?

Me: Ha! These HYPOTHETICAL associations are stored in cognitive nodes, which play an integral part in the Social-Cognitive Model of Transfe—

Black: Waittt...wait...see—you got too heady again! Bring it back! What is the Social-Cognitive Model of Transferring?

Me: Trans-ference...essentially, it says that we create mental representations of people or groups of people we find emotionally or motivationally significant to ourself, based on experience. We then store these associations into our memory. When we meet new people or encounter new ideas, we "transfer" this information into our representations of these new people in order to categorize, associate, and identify them in relation to ourself.

Black: Oh, okay, just like the Green person did with the Blue passenger...but what does that have to do with "Nommo"?

Me: Remember how Nommo, the spoken word, carries a universal life force, Ntu?

Black: Yeahhh...

Me: When someone initiates a conversation, especially by introducing himself or herself, the words spoken causes a mental activation in the listener's mind. There is a social and cognitive transference that triggers a cascade of mental representations in the listener or listeners that will affect the spiritual or psychological harmony the audience creates with you!

Black: Uhhh...I think I get it...

Me: Think about the N-word...I don't feel comfortable saying the full word, but do you know what I'm referring to?

Black: Yeah, N.I.G.G.E.R...one of the most vilest words ever created.

Me: Correct, that one. Why do you think that six letters—think about that…just six letters—can cause so much pain, misery, and trauma for an entire race of people?

Black: That's easy…because of the violence we associate with that word…the systemic violence, that's why we say NIGGA…to strip away the association of NIGGER. We strip the "ER," so we can strip away the colonizers' tools of oppression.

Me: Yes! Certainly! But on a psychological level, the N-word also strips away Black history and culture. When a listener hears the N-word, cognitively speaking, Black people are no longer the people of Niger, they are…that word. They are no longer associated with the Negus rulers of Ethiopia, they are associated with…that word. The terror of the N-word is that it erases the collective identity of an entire culture. But consider, though, that while "NIGGA" does not have the same malicious connotation as its predecessor, it can also be detrimental in a way. "NIGGA" eliminates the negative associations of N.I.G.G.E.R, but "NIGGA" doesn't insert an indisputable positive mental association to replace the negative associations of "NIGGER." The word "NIGGA" neither negates nor affirms a collective Black identity because there is no general consensus on what a "NIGGA" is. Thus, when non-Black people hear or think of "NIGGAS," they are left to their personal experiences to categorize and associate Blackness with whatever transference their cognitive nodes have mentally stored.

Black: Yes, but I can't worry about what associations people have of Black people. I would drive myself crazy!

Me: I am not saying you should worry, but you should be concerned. For most people, especially Americans, English is their primary language and in the English language, every word must fall into a part of speech… every word must have a purpose.

Black: Yeah, nouns are always subjects, verbs are always actions, adverbs describe verbs or other adverbs…so, what is your point?

Me: My point is that, if a word in the English language doesn't have a grammatical "function," then it doesn't exist. When a word like "N.I.G.G.A" is created and its "function" is not specified, a sort of psychological angst is created in the listener. It's like the Dogon described—without a name, you cannot exist.

Black: But why should I care if the oppressors think I exist or not? Why do I have to concern myself with their perception? Or with the associations of an abuser? Why is the responsibility on me to change the oppressors' mind? It just doesn't seem fair!

Me: It's not fair, but it's the "work." What I was trying to explain to you earlier is that, when you shift your focus from the "impact" to the "intent," you can start to understand why the attack is happening—where the attack is psychologically coming from. This understanding is the first step towards healing and only when we are healed can we move on and perhaps, one day, forgive.

Black: Woah, slow down…we a long way from forgiveness…

Me: When survivors of trauma escape their abuse, it's common for them to fall back into the cycle of abuse that caused the abuse in the first place. This cycle leads to maladaptive behaviors, which, in turn, leads to low self-worth and self-loathing because the pain and abuse feel more familiar to them than the love does. The survivors' self-concept, their "cognitive node," has connected to negative or restrictive affirmations and, consequently, they become the toxicity they've tried their whole life to escape. The only way to eliminate residual internalized toxicity is to forgive. Start by forgiving yourself and remember that your suffering is not your fault. With this understanding, you leave space for compassion and growth. Not just for yourself, but for your allies and maybe even your "enemies." Remember, the line between ally and enemy is thin. Your enemies are just allies in too much pain to know how to show up for you. Mostly because they are not showing up for themselves...

Black: See...I don't fully believe that...there are people out there that just hate and will never be my ally, no matter what I do! They won't be happy until I'm gone! They can't even admit that "I" matter...that "WE" matter; why can't they just admit that? I mean, how much more fucking basic can you get?

Me: Hmmm...so, you are saying that every Black person matters, regardless of who he or she is? If they are Black...they matter.

Black: Absolutely! For too long, they have tried to criminalize us, sexualize us, infantilize us, politicize us, divide us so that we hate ourselves, so that we can turn on each other, but I'm not going to do that...I love all of my people.

Me: I don't doubt your sincerity, but, just so I'm clear, you are saying that someone like Candace Owens, for example, who has been vehemently critical of you, her life matters?

Black: Huuhhh...yessss...even Candace.

Me: What about R. Kelly?

Black: Cancelled, but yes.

Me: What about Idi Amin? Who was known as the butcher of Uganda for killing hundreds of thousands of people in 197–

Black: I see what you are doing, and I don't appreciate it.

Me: What am I doing?

Black: You are gaslighting me. You are using my words against me so that you can discredit and dismiss my premise and, subsequently, my identity. But you can't dismiss me because I am not debatable...every Black life matters because Black people are living beings and every being has value: ergo BLACKK...LIVES...MATTERR.

Me: But by that logic, you have proved that Black people have value but not necessarily that they matter.

Black: You're nitpicking over semantics to make a point, so you can go fuck yourself!

Me: I've offended you?

Black: Ya think?

Me: Let's dig deep into that...let's say, hypothetically, that every person, regardless of culture, creed, or race...all sincerely conceded that Black lives do indeed matter. Would that quell some of your angst?

Black: It's literally the minimum...a baby step of a start.

Me: Ok, well let's take it even further. What if you and all other influential Black movements and Black leaders formed a union that was one of the most respected and powerful economic, cultural, and social forces in the world.

Black: Okkkayyy.

Me: And, as socially and politically progressive as this union was, a quarter of the constituents were homophobic, a third were misogynistic, and a few exploited the labor of children to—

Black: Okay, so where are you going with this? Yes, Black people are PEOPLE like everyone else. They are not perfect, but the rotten ones would get cancelled, read to filth, and dealt with because it doesn't matter who you are, wrong is wrong and an injustice anywhere is an injustice everywhere.

Me: So, what you are saying is that though these constituents have value to you, since they are Black…if you found their behavior or conduct inappropriate, their relevance to you would shift at your discretion?

Black: Not just my discretion…our discretion…as in the majority's discretion.

Me: So, if I understand correctly, a person or group of people's relevancy corresponds with how well they align with your values, morals, and purpose. Meaning that, how much a person matters depends on how you interpret their relevancy to you and the well-being of the social group you identify with. Simply put, "mattering" can be relative and subjective based on the observer because, per your own example, your own Black constituents matter to you only in as much as they coincide with your own values and vision.

Black: What's your point?

Me: So, if you, as a Black person, can debate or alter how much another Black person "matters"…can you see how a White person or even a non-Black person not particularly knowledgeable of your history or experience might be hesitant to proclaim your relevancy to them?

Black: You know what I was just thinking? That I was thirsty. Do you have a cup so I can drink all of these White tears? If folks can't get off their ass to read a book, watch a video, educate themselves, or simply just take a break from being ignorant long enough to witness the Black excellence displayed in their face every day, that's not my problem!

The whole world has exploited Black labor, culture, and creativity for its profit for hundreds of years. How could it not know how much we contribute to society?

Me: Well, a horse has historically been useful. The horse's labor has contributed to mankind's travel, food, and farming, among other things, but we don't say that "horses' lives matter" because usefulness does not necessarily equate to relevancy.

Black: Wowwww, did you really just compare Black people to farm animals?

Me: No, no, please don't misunderstand. I provide that example not to diminish Black people or your point but to point out that content without context can sometimes detract from the power of a message. You are not obligated to explain WHY you matter to people, but without explaining HOW you matter, you leave it up to others to interpret your relevance to them. And since the nature of interpretation is subjective, you unfortunately cannot control people's perception of you...for better or for worse.

Black: But how can the survival of Black people, the lives of Black people, be such a point of contention for so many people?

Me: I don't think that the contention is inherent, but with that being said, it is on you, the messenger, to make your message so clear, so concise, and so comprehensive that it is not just beyond reproach but it is perceived as unabashedly constructive.

Black: Hmmmm...I don't know...

Me: Let's take the "defund the police" policy as an example. It is not clear what systemic issue is being solved. Not to mention, what the side effects of defunding the police would be. The context of the content is not intuitive, and psychologically speaking, it affirms through negation.

Black: "Affirms through negation"?

Me: When one says, "I will gain something, if you lose something," as opposed to "we all gain because of what I can offer," a violent reaction is invoked in the mind of the recipient because there is a superficial perception of threat. This is not dissimilar to Martin Luther King, Jr.'s "Poor People's Campaign." When he changed the conversation from civil rights to economic equality, his message changed from prosperity through equality to prosperity through redistribution. "Civil rights" communicates that if you give your citizens equal opportunity to be contributors to American society, they will be. But when you suggest a redistribution of wealth or economic equality, the listener hears the speaker saying that, "I will become richer if the wealthier become poorer." I will AFFIRM my goal by NEGATING yours. Unfortunately, the discomfort associated with this message contributed to Dr. King's untimely demise.

So, when you make statements like, "defund the police," you leave an opening for detractors, like the Black conservatives, to accuse you of "Negation." Critics like Candace Owens don't need to fully understand the content behind your message because the presentation of your message allows the receivers to subconsciously attach whatever understanding they have of "defunding" on to your agenda.

Black: I know we are supposed to believe women, but that is the one woman I don't believe…"time's up" for that chick.

Me: From the little I know of Candace, it seems as though she grew up with her share of adversity. Sometimes, when a person grows up around trauma, particularly a person who is highly emotional or sensitive to stress and anxiety, that person can generalize the cause of that trauma to the groups of people that are closest to him or her—that they culturally or geographically identify with. Not unlike other ethnic groups, a Black person is susceptible to generalizing about the people he or she lives closest to—other Black people.

Have you heard of system-justification theory?

Black: No, what is that?

Me: System justification theory is the non-conscious tendency to defend and even augment the societal status quo, even when that status quo is detrimental to aspects of your identity. This occurs a lot with formerly colonized countries. Their culture has been destabilized by the colonial force for so long, they often cling to traditions and customs of their colonizers instead of their own culture. That's because that status quo is more understood and more psychologically stable than the uncertainty of change, even if the change is in their best interest. Thus, they "justify the system." Candace and other Black conservatives want to feel safe, to feel secure at all costs, even at the expense of parts of their Black identity.

Black: Candace has Stockholm Syndrome. She is in love with her captors and she thinks that if enough White people are "nice" to her, they will see her as one of them. She believes in the myth of meritocracy. She believes that if you smile, work hard, and don't complain about their abuse of you, then eventually you will earn their respect. Eventually, you will earn equity in the American dream. But it doesn't work that way. It doesn't matter how hard we work or how much we've overcome. We cannot be treated equally because we are not viewed as equals. And if they don't see us as equals, the only thing left to do is to change the frames.

Me: And that's the rub! Right there! You, Black, represent disruption, revolution, and change. Thus, you pose an implicit threat to Candace she may not have even consciously processed yet. Something to consider is that, as a leader, you are not obligated to indulge her behavior towards you, but I would encourage you to at least understand where that behavior rooted so you can eventually come to peace with it.

Black: I know where it is rooted…in some bullshit.

Me: Okay…let's backtrack a little here. She is a conservative, right? Aren't Black conservative platforms similar to other conservative platforms: low taxes, big business, traditional values?

Black: Yeah…

Me: That sounds like a page from—ohh, gosh, what was his name—Benjam…no Bo—

Black: Booker T. Washington.

Me: Yes, that's it, that sounds like a page from the Booker T. Washington page to me. And you seem more from the DuBois school of thought?

Black: I'm really triggered and uncomfortable that you are equating my mission with Candace's. I show up for my people…she sells them out. She is no better than Kanye West…tokenizing their Blackness so that White people can love them…why do you think both of their spouses are White?!

Me: Let's explore that. A person like a Candace Owens or a Kanye West is an American, just like you, which means that their cognitive nodes might habituate more to the core values linked to their "American" identity more than their "Black" identity. You say that the American justice system is broken, but don't you pay taxes to this "system"? Don't you speak the "system's" language"…pray in the "system's" churches? So, from an outsider's perspective, at least on paper, it would seem you also contribute to the problem. Is it soo unbelievable that African-Americans would cling to the American parts of their identity as much as the other identities linked to their self-concept?

You have to remember, someone like Candace Owens can create her own narrative of you, and, in her case, a negative one, because your key messages are not always as intuitive or as clear as you might think they are. Ambiguity in messaging can lead to confusion and confusion can lead to a disunified front.

Black: I feel like all I stand for is unity. If someone wants to argue about how much I "matter," that's on them, but if you cannot unify under "Black," then I can't help you.

Me: Funny you bring that up; I was meaning to ask you about that.

Black: About what, exactly?

Me: Your name…well, your first name—Black.

Black: What about it?

Me: Well, the term "White" as a racial classification first came about in the seventeen hundreds in British colonies in North America, but "Whiteness" has shifted boundaries and nationalities since then.

Black: Why are we talking about White people?

Me: Because my point is that you can't talk about Whiteness without talking about Blackness…Blackness cannot exist without Whiteness.

Black: What do you mean?

Me: Consider that the racial group "White" was defined as anyone without a drop of African or Indian blood…anybody that was "pure" from the "degeneracy" of Blackness. Later in the early twentieth century, "White" was used as a political construct to solidify power among European immigrants. They solidified this power to control and dominate descendants of Native Americans and African slaves. My point is, that you have chosen to identify yourself by a word that is defined by negation. Black is implied to be an antithesis to White, so when you say that Black…well…matters, you are saying, psychologically speaking, that everything that White people are not and don't want to be MATTERS. Instinctively, that affirmation is too uncomfortable to accept.

Black: I am just so SICK and TIRED of having to constantly justify my existence to EVERYONE…ALL THE TIME! Of my proving my worth ALL THE TIME, of proving that I matter ALL THE TIME! I'm tired of being strong…I'm tired of being resilient!

Me: Hey, hey! It's okay, it's okay…you have been through a lot, so you can give yourself permission to be hurt, to be angry. The key is to not turn the anger into hate because when you become hateful, you lose. You lose yourself because hate only attracts more hate, like a fire. If you don't direct that fire outward, it will go inward and continue to burn you up inside. Let the anger become fuel to propel you to a better place, a place of action and reconciliation, but if you pour the gasoline of hatred into you, you will get burned out.

Listen, I want you to repeat after me…c'mon, I know it feels weird but you can do it, it will help…I promise…repeat after me, I am more than enough…inhale…I am more than enough…exhale…good, now say it to yourself.

Black: I am more than enough, I am more…than enough.

Me: You don't owe anybody anything but your best, but do yourself a favor. Give yourself permission to be human, so that you can feel human again. Alrightttt? Feel better?

Black...

Me: Okay, now I'm going to ask you to do something for me. I want you to help me, help you.

Black: Okay Iyanla… how are you going to "fix my life," haha?

Me: This week, I want you to try an exercise. Okay? I want you to review every policy, label, protest sign, and name you go by and ask yourself if your message is affirming or negating. Take inventory of any negative or unclear messages and get rid of them. The ultimate goal of this task is for you to surround yourself with so many positive affirmations that you are shielded from the toxic projections of others. Optimally, by the end of your exercise, everybody won't just know HOW you matter, but, more importantly, you will unequivocally know how you matter, as well.

Black: But how do I decipher if a message is "affirming or negating"?…. It sounds kind of abstract.

Me: haha…I can be that sometimes. I hesitate to explicitly direct you because I would like this exercise to be a journey of self-exploration, but I can say that self-healing is always a good place to start. Heal yourself and then heal your community. Healing will give you the strength to find and create vehicles of positive affirmation and self-sufficiency. And the good news is that you seem to be well on your way!

Remember Black, no one can take away your story, your creativity, and, most importantly, your spirit! You have to keep your inner fire alive so your allies, your critics, and even your enemies have no choice but to gravitate to your warmth.

Black: Or to my smoke….

Tape Stops

> "Whewww, that was a long one…I hope they continue growing…okay, what do I have here…ohh, that's right, I'll have to hear this one again to believe it…Alright, got my second cup…kids are asleep, one more tape to go…"

■   ■   ■

Presses play…fast forwards…and recording of "Diversity August 19th Recording" plays

Me: Oh, uhh, hello. I didn't see you come in…huh—that's weird. Did the receptionist let you in?

Visitor: No, no, I just let myself in…Hope that's okay. I think you were out or something…are you free?

Me: Uhh, sure. I guess I can finish my lunch a bit early. Let's see here, let me just check my schedule and double-check if my afternoon is clear…

Visitor: It shoul—I mean, I sure hope it is…

Me: Hmmm, I guess you are right. It also looks like I kept my recorder on from the last session, so I guess we can just get started then…I'm sorry, I didn't catch your name. What was it again?

Visitor: Uhhh…Diversity! My name is Diversity.

Me: Diversity, huh? Haha, okay, that's a new one. Haven't heard that one before, but everybody seems to have some new a way of identifying themselves these days. But, still, that is very unique, reminds me of the seventies…Haha! Your parents must have spent a lot of time at Woodstock, huh?

Diversity: Yeah, I never really knew my parents...they weren't around much growing up. They were always kinda...distant.

Me: Sounds hard. Did you have a rough childhood?

Diversity: I mean, I was a bit of a hothead...but I learned to chill out, you know. Go with the flow. Go where the wind blows and sometimes where it doesn't.

Me: Hmm...okay...well, family dynamics can be tricky...is that what brought you in today?

Diversity: No, no, I've been having trouble sleeping lately. Like, for a while now...I've just on edge, ya know??

Me: Is that why you keep looking at your phone?

Diversity: Ohh, haha, woah...you're good, man. I didn't even notice that.

Me: It's pretty common, actually. In the age of technology, screens have replaced bibles.

Diversity: Woahhh, what does that even mean??

Me: Well, think about it. Since the creation of the modern printing press in the fifteenth century till the early twentieth century, the most consistently printed and sold books have been the Farmer's Almanac and the Bible. Now, in the twenty-first century, we consume information digitally, which enables us to diversify our access to various types of information. Consider that when we look at our phone, our iPad, or our computer—what direction do we look? Down. When we read the Bible, what direction does we look? Down. When we pray, we bow our heads and look...down. Checking our tablets has become a sort of ritual for us…a prayer to a newer god, a "better" god because we don't serve it, it serves us.

Diversity: Duuuddde, that's deep. What if the reality we are experiencing is just a hologram!! Wait, wait…just think about it! When you watch a movie, right, you are watching, like, a projection, like a three-dimensional world. Like our reality now, but it's not really happening. It's just on a two-dimensional piece of film that someone is playing. Maybe our galaxy works similarly to a movie screen playing on the surface of a black hole, but instead of a three-dimensional world on a two-dimensional film…it's like a four-dimensional world on a three-dimensional film.

Me: That is certainly an interesting theory.

Diversity: Crazy, right! Like, is that a piece of your mind on the floor over there?? Because it's been blown! Haha…think about it! Like, what if this all just like as simulation, you know? Like none of THIS was reallll!

Me: Like "The Matrix"…haha?

Diversity: EXACTLY like the MATRIXXX. There is this guy, uhhh, gosh… what was his name…ughh, this happens all the time…ummm oooo ooo Bostrom! Nick…I think is his first name. Do you know him?

Me: Can't say that I do.

Diversity: So, he's like a philosopher or something at…uhhh… Cambridge??? Oxford?? Some place where, like, really smart people go and he has these like farrr out ideas, man. He's all like, "what if none of our existence is, like, real." What if we are all extinct right now and the technology we created evolved past us. And future civilizations started running simulations of ancient humans so that they could, like, learn from people's mistakes and stuff. It's pretty gnarly stuff; you should check it out.

Me: Well, the concept of a "simulated reality" is not quite new. Plato famously described the empirical world as an "illusion." He proposed that humans are analogous to prisoners in a cave who confuse shadows of people projected onto a wall as actual people existing outside of the cave.

Diversity: That's trippy.

Me: Yes, "trippy, indeed." Almost two thousand years later, Rene Descartes followed up this line of thinking by saying that the whole world is a "deception," that the only thing any person can be sure of is that you are a "thinking being."

Diversity: I'm not even sure I am "thinking" most of the time…Ha!

Me: Speaking of your thoughts, and I don't mean to be presumptive, but I am a licensed medical professional, so I need to make sure that you are not any harm to yourself or anybody else…so, I have to ask: are you under the influence right now?

Diversity: Under the influence of what? You? Well, I guess. We just met, but you seem pretty influential…

Me: No, no. Are you intoxicated?

Diversity: Oh, am I high? Haha…nahhh, I'm actually as grounded as I've been in a long time! I'm just kinda tired.

Me: Well, sleep deprivation can cause some hysteria…so I guess that makes sense.

Diversity: So are you saying that if I stop looking at my phone, I'll be able to sleep better?

Me: Well, actually, yes! But I'm more interested in WHY you keep looking at your phone...

Diversity: Because I can't stop like...waiting.

Me: Waiting for what?

Diversity: For the next death, the next tragedy, the next disaster! This pandemic has shook up the world, you know!? Exposed how vulnerable people and the physical and theoretical structures they rely upon are. I know humans are the cause of this deadly virus and while people have been hurting Mother Earth for a long time, she usually doesn't hold a grudge for too long, ya know? I just feel like people are not coping well. Not adapting quickly enough and like all of the global instability and uncertainty has caused humans to do more harm to, like, themselves.

Me: But, there have been pandemics far more catastrophic than this one before and we have survived, so why the worry?

Diversity: But now, we are like one, though! People have never been as interconnected as they are now! Which makes any local conflict a global conflict! Conflict leads to a bunch of bad stuff, bro: lack of employment, lack of food, lack of water, lack of health, lack of education, lack of equality, and a lack of equality leads to instability. When there is instability, there is war. And I'm like totally anti-war, you know?

Me: Unfortunately, war is an unavoidable reality for humans. But, as horrific as war is, unless you are in one, it's nothing to literally lose sleep over.

Diversity: But there haven't been wars like this, man. It's like on another level! Like some dude named Bill working as a computer operator in a building office in Idaho could fly a drone to a village from another part of the world and wipe them out before he has his breakfast! Or a nuclear bomb could, like, blow up at any time and wipe out an entire civilization…and more than a dozen countries have them! And these nations are not cool with each other! Even scarier, dude, is the fact that biological weapons, that cause, like, mass murders, can be created and dished out to whomever…by ACCIDENT! So, the better question is… how are YOU sleeping well!!??

Me: Because, Diversity, I focus on what I can control.

Diversity: Control is a dream, man.

Me: Is that why you desire to go back to sleep? So, you can feel in control again?

Diversity: I want to sleep so I can have some peace. Peace of mind… all the time…is what I always say, haha.

Me: Well, I will do my best to help. When did this restlessness start?

Diversity: I don't exactly remember…it feels like it's been a while now.

Me: And how can I help? Sleep and mood disorders are not really my specialty. Why did you come to me?

Diversity: Well, I heard a rumor that you had the President as a client. I figured, if you can figure him out, you must be good!

Me: I can neither confirm nor deny.

Diversity: I think I really just need someone to talk it out with. If I could just understand why all this bad stuff is happening, maybe I will understand how to be at peace with it, ya know?

Me: Hmmm, okay, what are some of the conflicts you don't understand?

Diversity: Well, the way I see it, throughout history, humanity has been in this, like, constant struggle for power, right? They are like obsessed with it! And the "tug-of-war"…you see what I did there? Tug-of-war is like a kid's game but also people fight a lot. I write poetry in my spare time. But you get it, right?

Me: Yes, Diversity, let's try to stay on track.

Diversity: Right, right. So, there is, like, this constant struggle between the powerful and the powerless, the oppressor and the oppressed, the ruler and the ruled, the privileged and the marginalized, the conservatives and the progressives, the old and the young, the old and the new. This struggle creates more destruction than life! This idea that you need "power" to acquire resources is just an illusion, man—created by people who have never had enough natural or biological resources to survive. It's an illusion built out of insecurity…out of fear. Power is only useful when it helps ensure, like, peace and prosperity. The only reason you would fight over power is to either:

- Force someone to share his or her resources, because you don't have enough
- Take another's resources because you can't create your own
- Control others so that they don't waste the availability of limited resources or, even worse, take your resources!

Soo, in those circumstances, like, yeahhh…I GET IT…I guess. But you can avoid all of these situations! Humans can be each other's greatest resource as long as they organize land, food, and shelter in a way that everybody is responsible for themselves and their family—kinda like one big co-op! Then, they can eliminate the need for power altogether! Did you know that before the agricultural revolution, you know, before there were like "civilizations," people were hunter-gatherers. They were foragers, nomadic, adaptable, and self-sufficient! As far as I know, there was no systemic racism then. No political uprisings, no colonial oppression, no genocides. Self-organization works for every other animal on earth! Why can't humans get with the program!?

Me: What do you mean by, "It works for every other animal"?

Diversity: I'm talking about co-evolution, bro! When you leave species to worry about themselves.

Me: You do know that humans are the same species, so human conflict is therefore not 100 percent analogous to interspecies conflict, right? Many people in history have tried to equate different races with different species before, and history has not been kind to them.

Diversity: Yeah, yeah, no disrespect intended! For sure…for sure, but, like, there's a lot of overlap. Just trust me. Trust me, I promise I'm going somewhere with this.

Me: All right, I'm listening.

Diversity: So, like I was saying, co-evolution is this idea that species increase their chances of survival FROM interspecies conflict because if a species can't learn to biologically adapt to conflict…it dies. Historically, when animals self-organize, their struggle for survival facilitates a faster and more resilient evolutionary process. It's kind of deep if you think about it, bro.

Me: I'm a little rusty on my biology…can you elaborate on this concept of co-evolution a bit more?

Diversity: No worries, man, I got you…Alright, let me think of a good example…uhhhh…oh…alright. Let's say you have a traditional predator-prey relationship, right? Like a wolf andddd I don't know, like, whatever wolves eat. Okay?

Me: Okayyy.

Diversity: So, the wolf develops all these kind of bad-ass hunting skills: like a super sense of smell and like flesh-ripping teeth so it can devour and track down its prey. And then on top of all that, they hunt in packs so they can easily flank their prey if they try to escape! Crazy, right? Like who's gonna survive a wolf attack with all that, right? Alright, anyway, the pronghorn says, hey, Mr. Wolf! You might be able to, like, rip me to shreds but you'll have to catch me first! And, as a result, the pronghorn is the fastest animal in North America! Catch me if you can, right!

And then there are the eagles! They are like, we are not gonna run after you! We'll just swoop down and scoop you up! So, they develop this sharp eyesight and prey-gripping talons. And in response, or maybe in preparation…I don't know—it's honestly the proverbial chicken or the egg—tree insects and small rodents develop camouflage and aposematic—

Me: Aposematic?

Diversity: Oh, sorry, my bad. It means like distinctive coloration or markings to warn off predators, like a skunk or a monarch butterfly. It's similar to the adaptation of Mullerian and Batesian mimicry…

Me: Again, I study people…not as good with other animals. Haha.

Diversity: Oh, that's soo funny! I'm like really into nature and stuff. But, anyways, bees and wasps are Mullerian because they have developed the same color pattern on purpose to avoid being eaten by predators. The Scarlet snake or some King snakes are Batesian because they are non-venomous but "mimic" the coloring patterns of Coral snakes, which are highly venomous. Super bad news if you get bitten by one of those suckers. Haha…get it?…suckers because they suck your blood but they are also—

Me: Diversity, I get it. Ha, please continue.

Diversity: Right, right! So, yeah. But some animals avoid conflict altogether! Those are my favorite! Like why fight, man? Let's just live together in peace! Did you know that brown bears, musk oxes, and big-horned sheep are, like, these ferocious, strong mammals but only eat plants?! Imagine, like, Dwayne "The Rock" Johnson only eating salads. Awesome, right!?

Me: I guess…

Diversity: But, it's not just mammals—roses have thorns to avoid handling, grapevines have tannins, and—

Me: It's impressive how much you know about plants and animals, but what do they have to do with humans?

Diversity: Because, these animals didn't need civilizations or social constructs like race or gender or nations to survive. They didn't need power. They just needed a way to protect themselves or get the resources they needed to survive. So why can't humans do that?

Me: Well, while pre-agrarian people avoided more modern conflicts like racism and political instability, they traded in these global issues for more local tribal problems.

Diversity: What do you mean?

Me: Well, let's take the Aryans, for example, a local tribal contemporary of the Indus Valley Civilization. After centuries of regional control of the Indus River Valley, the Harappans eventually fell to the Aryans because the Aryans were able to exploit the internal Harappan political divisions for their gain. Unfortunately, Aryan rule of the region was short-lived because they did not create a set of societal rules and norms that unified and regulated the region. Despite the Aryan's success in acquiring control of capital cities—Harappa and Mohenjo-Daro—the Aryans did not become more evolutionarily fit than the agrarian Harappans they conquered. My point is, that while co-evolution has some benefits on an individual or local scale, it usually leads to mixed results for established societies on more global scales.

Diversity: But how are the results "mixed"?

Me: Well, take Alexander the Great, for example.

Diversity: Oh, I think I know him! He is the guy that the play "Hamilton" is based off of, right?

Me: That's Alexander Hamilton. Alexander the Great was a Macedonian conqueror that lived a long time ago. He is famous for never losing a battle because he led a Greek army to conquer Asia Minor, the Levant, Syria, Egypt, Assyria, Babylonia, and Persia—almost three thousand miles of land in just thirteen years. When he died, his empire broke into three kingdoms: the Antigonids in Greece and Macedonia, the Ptolemies in Egypt, and the Seleucids in Persia.

Diversity: So what is the point of conquering all of those places if they were just going to break off into separate empires anyway?

Me: Hence…mixed-results! On the plus side, Alexander established Greek as the common language—a move that allowed more people to trade and communicate efficiently. He not only established more than twenty "Alexandrias," but some of these cities became incredibly influential. For instance, the Alexandria of Egypt was a major learning center and held one of the most impressive libraries in the world. On the other hand, hundreds of thousands of people died as a result of his conquest. So does the "co-evolution" of culture, communication, and trade generated by Alexander's conquest justify the death toll it took to achieve it? That's for you to decide.

Diversity: But, that's just one example—that doesn't prove that co-evolution doesn't work for humans!

Me: Didn't you ever hear the saying about history…repeating itself?

Diversity: I never really heard many sayings growing up…I was kind of a loner.

Me: It was a rhetorical question…Ha. The only other conqueror that rivaled Alexander the Great's conquest record was Genghis Khan.

Diversity: Chaka Khan's sister was a conqueror!? Talk about mixed results! I mean one sister is this talented musician and the other takes over—

Me: Diversity! They are not related! Not even a little bit. Plus Gengis Khan was a man. Although he does have more descendants than anyone else in history.

Diversity: Ahhh, so they COULD be related!!

Me: They are not.

Diversity: But they could—

Me: Anyways, I was saying that, in the twelfth century, the Mongols, led by Genghis Khan, conquered more land in twenty-five years than the Romans did in four hundred years! They controlled more than eleven million square miles—that's almost four times as much as Alexander the Great.

Diversity: Woah…so, I guess music DOESN'T run in the family.

Me: They ARE NOT RELATE—you know what…forget it. My point is that there was a lot of evolution that came about because of this "predator." The Khan empire had this fast pony express called the "Yam system." It invigorated Eurasian trade that had been depleted since the Silk Road. But it wasn't just goods that traveled; food and even ideas traveled. The Mongols were notoriously very liberal in regard to religion. They usually allowed people to keep their culture and traditions as long as they paid the Mongols taxes. As a result, the "prey" learned to evolve as well. Out of this conquest, nations like Russia and Korea were created to withstand Mongolian rule, and even dynasties like the Yuan dynasty in China, the Ilkhanate in Persia, and the Chagatai in Central Asia outlasted the traditional Khan empire.

Diversity: So, I guess the ends justify the means, huh?

Me: Did they, though? Genghis Khan has been linked to the murder of millions of people and, to top it off, the cross-cultural pollination generated by his empire's efficient trade system was also, at least theoretically, responsible for the spread of diseases like the Bubonic plague, which would end up killing tens of millions of people.

Diversity: Hmmm…I guess the Mongols were too "mean" to justify… but on a, like, cosmic scale, it sounds like cons counteract the pros, so, like, everything balances itself out, right?

Me: More like CANCELS out...Take the most recent example of this co-evolutionary cross-cultural pollination—colonization.

Diversity: Did you just do that on purpose? Crossing-cult-colin—that "C" thing was cool. Duuude...you got skills...we should like start, like, a writing circle or something...you could lead the meditations; I could—

Me: Diversity...

Diversity: Sorry, dude...totally listening.

Presses pause.

"Gotta pee, gotta pee, gotta pee! Alright...no more cups of coffee."

Presses play

Me: European colonizers have been one of the most successful "predators" in modern history. Their predation has led to a proliferation of western values like democracy, the English language, and enlightenment ideas of social and political organization. Concurrently, though, the native culture of European colonies—the "prey"—is often eliminated, and when you have a variety of countries with erased cultural identities, you get crabs in a barrel. A sort of pseudo race between the colonized to see who can get closest to the resources of the colonizer. The prey compete with each other instead of collaborating. This is the main issue with "human co-evolution." The competition it creates decreases humanity's collective resilience from, let's say, disease, famine, or natural disasters, because everyone is looking out for their own survival.

Diversity: But when you say, "natural disasters," it sounds like you are just talking about intermediate disturbances! They can actually be really good for—

Me: Intermediate disturbances?

Diversity: Oh, sorry, ecology term. So, let's say there is a place, like, I don't know…a forest! And, somehow, lightning struck a tree and there was a wildfire, and the whole forest burned down. Sad stuff, right?

Me: That's kind of an extreme example from someone who, I assume, hugs trees in his spare time…

Diversity: Ohhh, nice burn, dude…Haha! You see what I did there—burn…fire…anyways. So, this fire wipes out the entire forest, right?…and all of the critters that live there. But something miraculous happens…after a while, primary producers like bacteria or fungi come crawling in and start converting sunlight and water into energy. The plants and new heterotrophs use this energy to grow. Then, herbivores, like insects and squirrels, come strolling in to eat the plants. Finally, predators who prey on herbivores swoop in and, before you know it, you have a new and even more biologically diverse community than before! So sometimes, intermediate disturbances like a fire or natural disaster are unfortunate but can lead to way more biodiversity. And the more biodiversity, the stronger the ecosystem!

Me: Intermediate disturbances can certainly create diversity among humans but they doesn't necessarily cause stability, because there is no solidarity in response to the disturbance. While an intermediate disturbance would cause "biodiversity," there is no guarantee a functional social order would develop among the different groups of people. This lack of cohesion can lead to a sort of decreased evolutionary fitness in this human ecosystem. Simply put, we reduce our collective chance at survival as a species if we do not work together.

Diversity: Alright, I guess I see your point. Hmmm, let me think here…Ooooh, I got it! What about realized niches?

Me: What was that? Did you say you realized something about Nietzsche? I'm mean, I know that you are a little disappointed, but I don't think we have to go nihilistic about everythi—

Diversity: Haha…I don't even know what Nea-lism is…Haha. I didn't say Nee-chay or whatever you just said. I said "niche"…like the space you occupy with your competition that allows you to survive with the bare essentials…

Me: Ohh..that niche, haha yes, I'm familiar. I guess I was just projecting…I have to make a note of that…anyways, what about them?

Diversity: Well, you said the problem is competition, right? That's only competition for the best resources but not necessarily the minimal resources you need to survive. What if everybody just found their realized niche and just occupied it? It turned out well for the finches!

Me: Finches?

Diversity: You know, Charles Darwin, Peter and Rosemary Grant? No, doesn't ring a bell? Dude…they are, like, famous!

Me: How do you know who the Grants are but not know who Genghis Khan is?

Diversity: Dude, I was a Biology major…plus, I told you I'm sleepy! I don't even know what day it is!…Let's just move on, cool?

Me: Sure

Diversity: So anyway, there were these Galapagos finches, right? The type Charles Darwin discovered in the eighteen hundreds.

Me: I'm familiar.

Diversity: Awesome! So, there was this species of finches, Geospiza Fortis, that was just chilling, minding their own business…livin' that easy-breezy island life…and then, BAMMMMM!!! Here comes Geospiza Magnirostris! With their big beaks and their big jaws just sucking up all the food! Disrespectful, man…dis-re-spect-ful.

Me: So, what happened?

Diversity: Well, Geospiza Fortis played it cool, they know they couldn't fight Geospiza Magnirostris. And they couldn't reproduce as fast as Magnirostris, so they just adapted! They realized their niche! It's like a whole thing that animals do! It's called character displacement! Twenty-two years after Magnirostris came along, the Fortis finches evolved to have smaller beak sizes so that they could get food in small, enclosed spaces that were harder for the big-beaked Magnirostris to get! That's the lesson for humans, man…you don't always have to compete for stuff all the time! Just decrease your beak and realize your niche! Great poem name by the way…gotta remember that.

Me: It does rhyme…I will give you that, but, more impressively, it does have precedents….

Diversity: What do you mean "precedents"?

Me: I just mean that it's happened before…with humans. In early Africa, those that did not want to compete for the plentiful resources migrated to other parts of the world. The ones that settled away from the equator needed less protection from the harsh equatorial sun. So, over time, the migrants evolved lighter skin and thinner hair to increase their exposure to vitamin D from the sun. Do you remember me talking about Russia earlier?? That country was created, in part, by the Mongols?

Diversity: Yeah…Chaka's sister.

Me: Uhhh, why do I even try? Well, the Muscovites of the Slav tribes survived the Mongols by inhabiting Moscow.

Diversity: Why is that a big deal?

Me: For two reasons: one, they could avoid the fallout from the fall of the Byzantine Empire and two, they were at the head intersection of four major rivers, which made Moscow a center for trade. So, this character displacement has been successful before, but—

Diversity: Noooo, not the "BUTTT."

Me: The problem is that all niches aren't created equal, and this inequity will inevitably lead to resentment and jealously. This jealously will eventually lead to fighting over the "best" resources. This is what happened to Harappa—

Diversity: Harappa?

Me: Do you remember the Indus River Valley civilization I was talking about earlier? That was displaced by the local tribes? Well, they herded cattle, which is a tough job! They were tired of the Harappans controlling the fertile farming lands near the Indus River and so…they took it.

Diversity: Dang…that's cold-blooded, man. No disrespect to Amphibians…just because snakes are poisonous doesn't mean all cold-blooded animals are harmful…frogs are qui—

Me: Diversity!

Diversity: I know what you are thinking and, yes, I did get lost in my thoughts for a second but I wasn't totally off track! I swear!

Me: Okay, prove it.

Diversity: What I was going to say, my good fellow, is that frogs use plants for protection!

Me: That…that was your ground-breaking statement?

Diversity: Dude, I'm talking about commensalism! Like when one organism just hangs out around another organism without harming it. Like a frog with plants, ya know? Or like…the remora fish! They have these literal and figurative "groovy" disks on their head that help them attach to larger animals. Isn't that sick, dude? They are like the ultimate hitchhikers because they never harm their ride. The remora fish just detach when they have to eat and wait for their next ride…living life like a highway…that's the way to do it, dude.

Me: Well, plenty of nomadic tribes like the Mongols actually did live peaceful, commensal lives outside civilizations…hunting and herding sheep and other livestock on the outskirts of cities. Benefiting from the proximity of the city without harming it.

Diversity: See! I told you Chaka's sister was alright!

Me: This was before Genghis Khan came into the picture. Wait—why I am even indulging th-…huhh, I'm actually glad you brought that up because the Khan nomadic tribes eventually desired to take over the resources and wealth of agrarian societies and well, you know the rest… war and pillaging.

Diversity: So, I guess that life isn't a highway…I can't believe that song would lie to me like that.

Me: I mean, I think it can be, but not if we lived like the remora fish. Then, our rides would probably crash and burn.

Diversity: Dude...dark! Well, alright...what if we just all worked together! That way, no bad vibes! No negative energy. No resentment! Just all work and all play! Everybody pulling their own weight like it should be!

Me: That's not the worst idea...there could be some issues with compensation, though...

Diversity: What do you mean? Everybody contributes and everybody benefits! Dude, do you know what an oxpecker is?

Me: From the name, I would assume an animal that pecks "oxen"?

Diversity: Woah, I didn't even think that...that's totally riggghhttt! These birds fly up to farms and just eat the ticks and flies. Just like all the little creepies crawlin' on the cattle!

Me: That doesn't sound mutual to me...

Diversity: Dude, what do you mean?! the cattle get, like, a free spa day! I'm talking grooming, manicures, pedicures...these cattle get free pest control!

Me: I don't know...still sounds kind of one-sided to me.

Diversity: Okay, okay...what about the bees and the flowers? Classic example! Beyonce receives nectar from flowers and the flowers get pollinated! Trust me, facultative mutualism is a total thing.

Me: I'm sorry, did you just say Beyonce?

Diversity: Isn't she the queen...of bees?

Me: Oh, my goodness...I don't even know where to start.

Diversity: Well, you can start by calling me a genius, ha ha.

Me: I will say that you are certainly…unique…but unlike you, facultative mutualism isn't unique…at least not among people.

Diversity: I don't know whether I should be happy or sad about what you just said.

Me: You are describing capitalism, at least the way Adam Smith intended it.

Diversity: Did you say "Adam Smith"—like I should know who that is? That is literally the most generic name I've ever heard.

Me: You, of all people, shouldn't be judging someone's name.

Diversity: Touche broheim…touche. So, what did John Doe say?

Me: Well, in one of the most influential pieces of literature in modern history, *The Wealth of Nations*, Adam Smith decrees that our individual need to fulfill self-interest results in social benefit.

Diversity: So, John thinks that we should, like, all be selfish?? That's totally not what I'm about.

Me: ADAM is saying that if everybody does what makes them happy, what they are good at, then we can create a web of interdependence which will eventually generate a sort of equilibrium of supply and demand. He called this the "invisible hand."

Diversity: Woah…equilibrium, interdependence, invisible hands! John Smith sounds awesome.

Me: Well, a lot of people do think ADAM Smith is "awesome," and capitalism does work most of the time, except when it doesn't. So, capitalism works when everybody can contribute labor of value and when an economy is supplying and demanding tangible and finite resources. But, when you have a market that trades IN-tangible goods and services like "credit," or "insurance," or "stocks," you run the risk of fraud and even corruption.

Diversity: I mean, it can't be that risky…

Me: The 2008 subprime mortgage lending crisis caused a global recession. Thousands lost their homes and millions lost their savings.

Diversity: Yeah, that is bad. Well, what if everybody was, like, dependent on each other…like the bacteria that live in hosts' intestines? The bacteria receive food and shelter and the hosts get better digestion and protection from microbes. Doesn't that sound like the best Airbnb to you? Like, if people knew that if that their survival was dependent on everybody else's survival, then humans could CAPITALIZE on these relationships. Eh eh…you see what I did there!? Adam would be proud.

Me: I'm just proud you got his name right!

Diversity: Dude, I ALWAYS remembered John Adams' name!

Me: Ughhh, if you force interdependence on people you don't have capitalism anymore because capitalism thrives on a FREE market and competition. What you have is communism or socialism.

Diversity: Commune…social…sounds good to me!

Me: Well, what you get in stability you lose in individual expression and diversity, which are indispensable ingredients of progress.

Diversity: Well, maybe there needs to just be one chef in the kitchen! Like, what if there was, like, one person whose whole job is to make all the decisions, ya know? And like everybody else, can just relax and chill and just live their lives!

Me: It sounds like you are taking about a dictatorship and, trust me, that never ends well.

Diversity: No, just hear me out! Humans are already parasitic because they receive all their nourishment from all the plants and animals in the world, without the plants and animals getting much in return. Humans can just model the relationship they have with plants and animals to a relationship where one or a few humans supply the rest of the humans with the nourishment the majority need. It's more common than you think, man...like more than half of the species on Earth are parasitic and, typically, if an ecosystem has parasites, then it is a healthy ecosystem!

Me: So, you know that one or a few people you gave all the power to make decisions? Well, historically speaking, once you give a person or a group of people unchecked power, they usually lose respect for human life. Have you ever heard of Joseph Stalin? He and his followers killed more than twenty-five million of his own people. Not for war or for profit but for control...because he could.

Diversity: Man...that is a bummer. This conversation is depressing, dude...I thought you were supposed to make me feel better! I think I feel worse than before I got here! Maybe we are all just doomed, man.

Me: Maybe, but maybe not...isn't there a guy who is trying to colonize Mars??? He owns Tesla...

Diversity: There is somebody who OWNS Nikola Tesla?? I thought slavery was outlawed? Plus, I'm pretty sure Nikola is dead...?

Me: No, the company...Elon! Elon Musk. He owns a private space shuttle company and one of his primary missions in life is to prepare Mars for colonization after the inevitable collapse of humanity.

Diversity: That's just a movie.

Me: What do you mean? He is always in the news.

Diversity: Wasn't he in *Æon Flux*? You know—2005, Charlize Theron, deadly pathogens, dystopian civilization...sounds like you are talking about another science fiction film. Why do you think he calls himself "Ironman" and named his child X Æ A-12...dude, he loves sci-fi flicks!

Me: Diversity, I assure you he is not an actor. He seems to have found a solution to humanity's limited resource problem. He wants to take a small group of us and start a new civilization—one with an overabundance of resources.

Diversity: Yeahhh, I don't know about that dude. So like, jeesh, I don't know...3.9 billion—maybe it was 3.5...it's kinda fuzzy, but yeah, sometime between 3.9 billion and 3.5 billion years ago, prokaryotes hopped on the scene and they had Earth all to themselves...just like that Martian dude wants to do, but here's what happened. Like, all of a sudden, around 2.3 billion years ago...the oxygen concentration in the atmosphere shot up to like 10 percent in, like, fifty million years!

Me: All of a sudden? How is fifty MILLION years all of a sudden?

Diversity: Dude...it's, like, all about perspective, you know? like how you look at things. Earth is billions of years old, so like fifty million is kinda like a second in time. Isn't that trippy to think about? How like time can be, like, different, depending on how you perceive it? Makes you think...is time even really, like, real? Or do we just think it's real because of its effect on us...woahhh!

Me: Diversity, focus! What caused the oxygen to show up?

Diversity: Uhhh, my bad, dude…alright, uhh, so yeah, 2.3 billion years ago, right. The oxygen in the atmosphere appeared because this new prokaryote called cyanobacteria figured out how to, like, make its own food from photosynthesis. Rad, right!?

Me: What does that have to do with oxygen?

Diversity: Well, because, dude, oxygen is created by splitting hydrogen ions from water molecules and when you take that H from that O, oxygen is just left, chillin' by himself. So, he gets all of his other single, lonely oxygen bros and, like, goes up to the sky to hang out. This is like how all life, like, breathes…it's pretty crazy.

Me: So, the oxygen revolution sounds like a good thing.

Diversity: Well, it was for us, all of the species that evolved after this oxygen-dependent cyanobacteria, but it was totally bad news for the cyanobacteria that came before this new cyanobacteria. See, the old-school cyanobacteria grew up on an Earth without oxygen—just carbon dioxide. So, when all of the CO_2 was being used to create oxygen…they couldn't adapt.

Me: So, what you are saying is that if a species lives by itself without other species, its chance of long-term survival is severely limited?

Diversity: Correctumundo, dude! Plus, what's wrong with Earth, man? She's a pretty special rock—why do humans have to leave it so soon? What if humans just have it out right here.

Me: What do you mean?

Diversity: What if we just let everybody do their thing and winner takes all, you know? Death-style cage match! Many enter...only one leaves! That way, whoever wins has the whole place to themselves, fair and square! It worked for the parameciums!

Me: What are parameciums? Is that another type of bacteria?

Diversity: No, dude, they are plants! If you leave Paramecium Aurelia in its own habitat and Paramecium Caudatum in its own habitat, everything is ALLLL good. But if you put them in the same habitat...it totally doesn't work. P. Aurelia outcompetes P. Caudatum for food, which causes P. Aurelia to reproduce a little faster than P. Caudatum. Just that little bit of advantage in reproductive rates will eventually bring about P. Caudatum's extinction! Which is, like, totally sad for P. Caudatum, but it's fair and P. Aurelia has the place all to herself!

Me: Well, the "fairness" you are talking sounds like sanctioned genocide.

Diversity: Woah, that's way too far...that's totally not what I meant.

Me: Well, it may not be what you meant, but it is what it would certainly lead to. In 1994, the Rwandan Civil War was generated because the majority Hutus were unhappy that the minority Tutsis controlled more valuable livestock. This class warfare resulted in the murder of almost a million people and, after all that bloodshed, the Hutus were not better off for it. It's like you said about cyanobacteria...live together or die alone.

Diversity: But I just don't understanddddd. Why does it have to be so hard? Like, every other species has learned to live together without causing mass destruction! The bison graze in herds. Herrings group in schools, birds of the same feather—

Me: Flock together?

Diversity: Woah, did you just make that up? Really clev—

Me: No, that's a very common say—

Diversity: Right, right, but it's not just that they flock together, dude; they work together! Check it out—birds, like, fly in an inverted V or J formation instead of lining up linearly. Why do they do that, you might ask? Because the formation gives each bird a clear line of sight and the wind current created by the flapping of the anterior birds makes it easier for the trailing birds to fly.

Me: But, doesn't this formation exhaust the leader in front? Who, because it's the leader, has no wind current from an anterior bird to carry its momentum?

Diversity: Dude, they alternate leaders…so that no individual bird gets too tired. Birds are really sharp, which is interesting, because people use the term "bird brain" in a derogative wa—OH, MY GOSH…I totally figured it out! I got it! I totally figured out the solution to every human's problems!

Me: Don't have any central leadership?

Diversity: Live like ANTS! It's perfect, dude! Check it out. Ants don't have any leadership, so there is no, like, power trip that you were talking about with that dictator-guy, Adolf Hitler.

Me: Joseph Stalin…you know what, it still applies. Carry on…

Diversity: Then, there is like one queen and she is the only female that can produce offspring, which solves the commensalism issue, because no one could take over her job out of, like, jealousy…or whatever!

Me: Okay, I'm with you so far.

Diversity: Then, with ants, there is task allocation. Everybody has a specific job and if, like, there is a flood or a food shortage or, whatever, they just change jobs based on whatever conditions change! It's like capitalism on acid, dude…just pure harmony. Then, speaking of chemicals, ants use chemical trails to show other ants the path they used to find food, and the best part is that they have developed all of these factors genetically, which means that humans could potentially evolve to do it, too!

Me: What do you mean "developed genetically"?

Diversity: Let me give you an example. So, remember how I told you how awesome birds were at flying?

Me: Yes, of course.

Diversity: Well, there is this theory, right: that birds didn't originally use feathers for flight…dude, think about that! Birds NOT flying! That's like fishes not swimming or, like, humans not walking. But, I guess, since all species came from, like, the ocean, you gotta start somewhere…

Me: Diversity…

Diversity: Right, sorry dude. So these ancient "birds" probably used these feathers to keep warm or to attract mates, right, but as the Earth got warmer, birds learned to use their feathers for better purposes—flight! The feathers were genetic exaptations passed down to their offspring over generations. The resulting phenotypic exaptation led to an increase in biological fitness for the modern aerial bird over other winged birds, like the penguin, because aerial birds can like fly, which is awesome. You with me so far?

Me: I think I'm following…

Diversity: Cool, so, like this ability to make use of old biological traits to organize and survive should theoretically be possible in humans, because they are able to generate so much genetic variation! Dude, there are, like, so many phenotypes and we, like, mix and match them all the time! Like a funky meiotic Rubik's cube! Perhaps humans can develop traits they don't need but could be used later to enhance their future offspring's survival?

Me: Sexual reproduction, asexual reproductions mutations, transcription errors, translation errors…not impossible, but humans are 99.9 percent similar, genetically speaking.

Diversity: Totally, dude, but did you know that since women have two X chromosomes, they often have, like, two genes that code for the same trait on different X chromosomes! Then something far out happens…in embryonic development, one of the genes on corresponding X chromosomes gets suppressed totally randomly! That's why there is all this genetic variation among women because this allele inactivation causes sporadic and abundant genetic variability. Isn't that gnarly, dude? That's why women should be leaders, dude…diverse biology…diverse problem-solving skills! Like, have you ever noticed, like, zero women have ever caused a genocide? Anyway…what was I saying?

Me: You were talking about genetic variation…but I'm not sure what it has to do with ants.

Diversity: Right, right…so, for humans, right…let's say, there is one gene for red hair and another for brown hair, but you also have a gene for baldness. If the "baldness" allele gets expressed, then it kinda doesn't matter what "hair color" traits get expressed. This epistasis causes, like, a tunnel after generations of reproduction.

Me: A tunnel?

Diversity: Yeah, a stochastic tunnel. Genes will reproduce in a way that eventually leads to the expression of the traits most optimal for survival. So, the more genetic diversity, the greater the likelihood of evolving the evolutionarily fittest gene. That's what's been totally happening with ants!

Me: What do you mean?

Diversity: Ants have been around for millions of years; humans have been on earth for only, like, two hundred thousand, which means that we should DO. WHAT. ANTS. WOULD. DO. Hehe.

Me: As opposed to do what Jesus would do?

Diversity: D.W.A.W.D…nice ring to it, right? I should totally copyright that, dude. If humans set up some reproduction guidelines, perhaps their genes will evolve like ants and they can live for millions of years!

Me: That is certainly a…strategic thought in theory, but it wouldn't work so much in practice.

Diversity: Woah, why not?!

Presses pause…

   "How much tape is left on this…halfway, huh…alright."

Presses Play

Me: Well, the ethical implications notwithstanding, people are not principally guided by their genetics. We have free will. We have choice. Ants and birds don't have the same frontal lobe size as us, so they don't mind following rigid or biological impulses of organization and survival. Humans can think for themselves. We can decide how we want to live our lives and what our individual life is worth, respectively.

Diversity: Like in respect to what?

Me: In respect to how much fulfillment we can acquire and how much suffering we can avoid. We organize our life in respect to life and death.

Diversity: But, that like doesn't make any sense! Are you saying that life is only worth surviving if humans can avoid suffering? Suffering is what compels people to survive!

Me: Yes, but there is a difference between suffering and struggling. We make policies that ensure people are not tortured in captivity. We are instinctively concerned when we see the inhumane conditions of abject poverty. We have pity on those who have gone through tragic circumstances because we recognize that the suffering is needless. That it might have been avoided. Whereas, struggling IS a part of the human condition, but we disagree on what struggles are necessary for fulfillment.

Diversity: But, what could be more fulfilling than, like, avoiding death? I thought humans' constant beefing over power was all about their need to survive? Or, do people only fear death because they associate it with suffering? Would humans fear death if death occurred without suffering? Woah...my head is starting to hurt...

Me: It depends on the culture, a society's philosophies, and an individual's personal beliefs.

Diversity: But, like, why the obsession with power, then? Power is only valuable because it helps you avoid death. If people saw death as, like, independent of suffering, then humans wouldn't obsess over power. But they DO obsess over power. So, death must be a total bummer. With that logic, death must be a thing that humans want to avoid at all costs!

Me: Just because we fear death doesn't necessarily mean that we want to avoid death. In many cultures, death is just seen as the next step in a journey of the soul or the next step in the transition between physical states. In these cases, fear is more of a reflex than a conscious avoidance.

Diversity: So, if humans are capable of not fearing death, why do they mourn the ones that died? If death is just a "transition," why be sad at all?

Me: Because we mourn the memories and experiences that we have missed out on due to the fact that the deceased are not here to experience them with us anymore.

Diversity: So why not mourn the people who have never lived?!

Me: "Never lived"?

Diversity: For all the billions of people who have lived, there are like trillions of people that never got to be born! Wild, right? That's trillions upon trillions of experiences that humans have missed out on! Isn't that, like, way sadder?

Me: Those who have not lived are not equivalent to those who have lived and died because the ones who have lived, however briefly, made an impact on the world, even if it was a minimal impact. Who knows how a deceased person's impact influenced the progression of the human species. Whereas someone who was never born, never had the opportunity to change the world in even the slightest way.

Diversity: Woah…okay, so are you saying that the worth of a human life ultimately comes down to its impact on the collective fitness of the human species?

Me: Yes.

Diversity: But, let this sizzle in your skillet…even if we reduce the importance of human life to impact…the impact could be good or bad, and if the impact is bad, a person's legacy could result in harm and even death. Isn't that the whole thing humans are trying to avoid?

Me: Yes, but deciphering what is "good" or "bad" for EVERYBODY, ALL THE TIME, gets complicated.

Diversity: Dude, what's so difficult about it? "Good" or "bad" people, behaviors, and ideas are just a spectrum of things that increase or decrease overall fitness for the greater goal—survival. Everything in the world falls on an advantageous/disadvantageous spectrum. If humans are specific about what attributes fall in this spectrum, they can work together to avoid disadvantageous circumstances!

In order to properly identify attributes that are disadvantageous, humans should avoid being distracted by totally superficial signifiers like phenotypic, racial, or cultural differences. Demonizing our enemies only puts you in hell, dude…that's what I always say.

Me: But there is a reason why we focus on differences. Biologically, they signal to us a real threat to the "ultimate goal of survival." Remember the coloring patterns in snakes you were talking about a few hours ago? I think they were Batesian or maybe Mullerian? I always get those confused! But the coral snakes are venomous and other snakes have evolved to mimic these patterns so they can take advantage, because oftentimes difference can be the difference between life and death.

Diversity: Difference is real, but the relevancy of this difference is subjective. Dude, something can be harmful to you, but necessary for survival, like getting flu shots. Alternatively, something can be good for you but not significantly helpful for your survival, like chocolate. Perception is about the frame you are observing it from, but if you add up all of humanity's differing perspectives, they equate to the same thing—survival. Some perspectives are constructive for survival and some are not, and humanity should praise what increases survival and avoid what doesn't. Ideally, the appearances of these differences shouldn't matter.

Me: Well, here on Earth, there is no way to know for sure if your behaviors or motivations are actually advantageous or just perceptually advantageousness. There have been so many crusades, jihads, and massacres caused solely by our perception of right or wrong—by our assessments' advantageousness and disadvantageousness. Everybody believes in something even if a person chooses to believe in nothing. As a result, discerning the value of certain differences over others becomes confusing and sometimes even dangerous.

Diversity: But, differences are not worth losing your life over! Like, dude, it is just not that serious! Uhhh…let me see…what's a good example…what's that over there?

Me: Oh, near the edge of my desk? It's just hand lotion.

Diversity: Aweessommmee, that's perfect.

Me: Perfect for what?

Diversity: My example, dude! Get popcorn and get comfortable! I want to tell you a story about your lotion…

Me: Oh goodness, this should be interesting.

Diversity: Dude, differences can be significant, but if you let yourself get caught up in them, you can miss out on some totally golden opportunities! Like, once upon a time…the Europeans were just doing their European thing—conquering and exploring things. And, for some reason or another, they invade the south-west Arabian peninsula! Mind you, Europe and Arabia have been, like, neighbors for centuries and throughout history, Europeans would look out at the arid, dry Arabian desert and wonder what could possibly survive out there. So, they took their guns and their soldiers and marched right past along these little green plants that had jagged teeth and were prickly to the touch.

The Europeans pitied the native Arabians, because their land was so seemingly desolate. So totally bare, with crops that they had to settle with "weeds." Little did the Europeans know, but was, like, common knowledge to North Africans, Canary Islanders, Cape Verdians, and, of course, Arabs, that this "weed" could heal burns, repair skin, and prevent diseases! On top of all that, dude, this magical plant needs very little water to grow and can survive in the harshest climates! It took the Europeans until the seventeenth century for a Dutch Botanist named Laurens Burman to figure out how awesome this weed was…and you know what he named this wonder plant? Aloe Vera! The main ingredient in your lotion, dude!

Me: But European explorers are not necessarily botanists…how were they supposed to know the properties of a plant that wasn't native to their land?

Diversity: Huh, alright I guess I gotta reach down in the ole treasure chest so I can find a jewel of an example that will convince you, dude! Alright…let me see here…annnddd look at that…we've struck gold! Buckle up my friend, you are about to get turned around!

Me: Click, click (imitates buckle-clasping noise)…what's the GPS set to?

Diversity: Let's take another example. Same time period, around the seventeenth century, but instead of Europeans going west to the Arabian Peninsula, let's go east to the Americas! Halfway across the world, Jesuit missionaries were "exploring" modern-day Peru and "saving" the Quechua people from their "backwards" and "primitive" religious practices.

Me: You can stop with the air quotes…the sarcasm is registered.

Diversity: Too much?

Me: Just a little…

Diversity: Aright, so, anyway, the Quechua were, like, total bosses at farming and cultivating crops. They grew the superfood quinoa.

Me: And carbohydrate-rich potatoes…

Diversity: That's exactly right, dude! How did you know that?

Me: It came up in a previous session, but please continue.

Diversity: Righteous…and speaking of righteous…the Quechua were so into plants that they worshipped them! Specifically, the quina-quina bark from the Cinchona tree! So, when the Jesuits strolled up to South America, they were like, "you Quechua dudes are sooo dumb. There is only one true God, and he definitely doesn't live in a tree!" And just like the aloe vera plant, it took hundreds of years later for the Europeans to figure out that the chemical element in the Cinchona bark has properties that treat malaria, babesiosis, lupus, and arthritis. They later called the medicine derived from this chemical quinine on behalf of the Quechua people! So, let me ask you. Was it primitive for the Quechua people to worship a mystical plant that cures deadly diseases in real time as opposed to a god that indifferently attributes their suffering to their inherently sinful nature? Superficial differences don't give someone the right to ignore or erase the value of another person's culture because difference is a mirage, mannn. We ARE ONE.

Me: But everybody is susceptible to these biases; it's not just the Europeans. Evolutionarily, we survived by our ability to take differences seriously. It's an efficient cognitive shortcut we use for survival. If a plant is green or vibrant in hue, it indicates ripeness and nutrition. Whereas, something that is brown usually indicates moldiness and bacteria.

Diversity: Fair point, fair point, but let's consider those religions and beliefs we were talking about earlier—that make deciding what's "good" and "bad" just sooo confusing. Don't you find it suspicious that the world's most popular religions have, like, the same elements to them?

Me: What do you mean, "the same elements"?

Diversity: Take some of the world's most popular religions, for example: Judaism, Christianity, Islam, Buddhism, and Confucianism.

Me: Alright…

Diversity: So, let's disregard the fact that Judaism, Christianity, and Islam all include the same patriarchal figure.

Me: Patriarchal figure…oh, do you mean Abraham?

Diversity: Exactly dude—in Judaism, he is, like, the head honcho!

Me: Are you saying that because he is the founding father of the covenant of the pieces?

Diversity: Right again, man! God just showed up one day and was like…"Hey, Abraham, all of your little dudes will get this sweet piece of land called Israel if you, like, do everything I say!" But what's crazy is that he shows up again in Christianity. The Bible says that Abraham is like the Michael Jordan of all believers! Or maybe LeBron James?? I mean, after that documentary, I'm really leaning toward Michael but—

Me: Diversity!

Diversity: Haha, my bad, dude.

Me: Back to your Abraham example. It makes sense that they share some commonalities because they share the Old Testament. Even Jesus was Jewish, so it makes sense there was overlap…

Diversity: But how do you explain Islam? Muhammad showed up, like, six hundred years after Jesus came around and said that this dude, Abraham, was a link in a chain of prophets that begins with Adam and ended with himself. Spooky, right?

Me: Not really. It would be more coincidental if Judaism, Christianity, and Islam occurred at the same time but existed in completely different parts of the world with no way of contacting each other and then described the same man in the same way. Now, that would be conspicuous.

Diversity: Alright, but how do you explain this? Abraham is, like, this older man with not much status or wealth, struggling to have a family but because of his faith and devotion to God…BOOM! He gets all this prime real estate that his juniors get to look after!

Then you have this regular carpenter with not much money and influence and because HE listens to God…BAM! gets a flock of devoted followers, and all these powers, like the ability to resurrect the dead, eat as much bread and fish as he wants, and just get drunk whenever! And because of Muhammad's devotion to God, the angel Gabriel appeared to this 40-ish-year-old caravan trader and was like, if you recite the word of God for me, I'll like totally make you the most power ruler of Medina and eventually Mecca! All of these stories have more in common than Abraham…dude, rub the genie lamp and presto! You will become this great, revered, and powerful dude…and didn't we say that humans are like obsessed with power? Sooo...it makes sense that they get totally hooked!

Me: Hmmm...yes, although monotheistic religions provide similar paths to empowerment, it doesn't necessarily prove that all religions are the same.

Diversity: Totally, dude, but even in religions that aren't strictly monotheistic, like Buddhism and Confucianism, the origin stories of their prophets are strikingly similar! The prophet usually leads a life of "earthly" privilege, only to leave it for a more righteous and spiritual path. Did you know Buddha was this wealthy guy who, like, rejected his big house and diamond chains?

Me: Diversity, you are getting carried away again.

Diversity: Sorry, dude, but you don't know! He sounded like a total baller! Anyways, Buddha left his fast life to fast...see what I did there?

Me: Yes, Diversity.

Diversity: Rad, so he leaves to pray and meditate and, because he chooses a path of redemption, he becomes "enlightened"—which, in Buddhism, is the like best thing you could totally be. Same thing with Confucianism! Kung Fu Tzu was a decorated politician, a statesman, I think...but because he chose to live "righteously," kings and emperors would follow his "mandates from heaven" for like hundreds of years!

Now that I think about it, it kinda makes sense that less deistic belief systems are a bit less popular than the more classical monotheistic religions. Not every believer is born rich and ditches wealth to get zenned out like Buddha. Also, having rulers follow your moral and ethical standards is not as sexy as BEING an actually ruler...but regardless of the amount of gods in a given religion, somehow the prophets are suspiciously always men around a certain age that tend to follow some type of divine will with a sense of devotion that they alone are privy to.

It's like in the "Make a Successful Religion" cookbook!

> Step 1. Get a regular dude.
>
> Step 2. Make him follow some righteous path ordained by some divine will.
>
> Step 3. Reward him for following the path.
>
> Step 4. Create a set of guiding principles and moral codes that are malleable enough to apply to any type of person in any stage of life, but also make sure these moral codes are general enough to be subsumed by the traditional practices of a given culture.
>
> Step 5. Let ethical guidelines cool for a couple of a hundred years.
>
> Step 6. And, finally, dig in! Haha!

There is a reason why Hammurabi's Code isn't on the *Times* Best Sellers List…"an eye for an eye" is way too specific. Now, if you said, as it does in Corinthians 15:58, "Therefore, my beloved brothers, be steadfast, immovable, always abounding in the work of the LORD, knowing that in the LORD your labor is not in vain"…you are finally cooking with grease! "The work of the Lord" could be applied to any "brothers" and to any "work" in any given situation!

Me: The reason why Hammurabi's Code isn't more popular is because it's not sustainable for kids to have their hands cut off when they have outbursts towards their parents.

Diversity: I'm totally picturing a group of kindergartners running around trying to play tag with no hands…woaahhh.

Me: You are so ridiculous, Diversity.

Diversity: But if you think about all the least popular religions that either didn't stand the test of time or remained locally worshipped belief systems, they had prophets or rulers that weren't relatable. The power of these less successful religions was usually "ordained" from God by a political figure, like the Roman Emperor Augustus, not for the empowerment of the weak and suffering like in the Quran. Augustus was like "My power was given to me by divine province, so all you dudes have to listen to me!" And, surprise…surprise, he got the boot from Constantine who established…..wait for it…wait for it…Christianity! Akhenaten is another good example who, like other pharaohs, became a ruler by a birthright gifted to him by some dudes who worshipped Aten. And can you guess what the current national religion of Egypt is??? Islam! Because no one likes some random dude hogging all of the access to God.

Me: Okay, Diversity, you've made your point…historically, people tended to engage in their belief systems predictably. That doesn't necessarily mean that their faith has been devalued.

Diversity: But survival has little to do with faith! Survival is about behaviors and humans haven't just behaved predictably throughout history—their behaviors remain predictable today! Think about it, if you take out the religious dogma, the moral/ethical rules, and the cultural traditions of worship…you have a cult-like devotion to a mythical hero…remind you of anything?

Me: I'm not really good at guessing games.

Diversity: The Avengers! Don't you think it's weird that if you drop the "t" from Christ you get Chris…as in Chris Hemsworth, who plays the superhero Thor? Or Chris Evans, who plays Captain America? Or Chris Pratt, who plays Starlord? Take out the Bible and the angels and prophecies from God but slightly change the origin story. Instead of a man immaculately conceived from Mary…make your hero immaculately conceived from a woman dying from cancer in Iowa in 1986 and you get Starlord! If you substitute Jesus's arch nemesis—the oppressive and "evil" Romans—for Nazi Germans, then you get Captain America. Instead of giving Christ the ability to manipulate the forces of nature, like walking on water or living forever, give an alien demigod the power to channel lightning and live like an immortal being and you get Thor.

The point is that the details around the story don't matter as long as the general premise stays the same! For the same reason, though, crusades, holy wars, centuries-old feuds, and even genocides have been waged over people's favorite superhero!

Me: Hmm, I understand where you are coming from, but even if the origin stories, as you say, are similar for the prophets when they were on Earth, that doesn't mean they have the same views on the places they went after they died.

Diversity: Sure, fine, but regardless of what afterlife or spiritual place someone believes in, what difference does it make when you are alive? Isn't survival the most important thing to live for while you are still on Earth?

Me: …

Diversity: See, all motivations eventually arrive at survival, so it is crucial for humans to organize themselves in a way that optimizes it!

Me: But, you do know that efficient and peaceful organization doesn't necessarily lead to a prosperous ideal society, because it is impossible to have a universal consensus on what is advantageousness and what is disadvantageous for survival.

Diversity: Fine, dude, if humans do not want to share the power or agree on what humans should do to survive, then the only alternative is to increase the amount of power there is. And the only way to do that is to increase the carrying capacity.

Me: And how do you propose we do that?

Diversity: The only way to do that is through technology, and the most optimal way of creating new technologies is to share resources so that humans can create incremental improvements to newer and newer ideas. Or, humans could totally increase the amount of varying perspectives on any given problem to increase the likelihood of creating solutions. See humans don't need power, they just need lots of different people and strategic vantage points working together to survive!

Me: Sounds good…theoretically.

Diversity: Theoretically!?? Dude, it's totally been done before…don't you know how monumentally awesome the steam engine was?

Me: Not exactly, but I'm sure you are going to tell me.

Presses pause…

"Now, this is where my memory gets fuzzy.. did I dream all of this? Am I dreaming now? Doesn't matter, almost done!"

Presses play

Diversity: Right, again! Get ready to hold your horses! Haha...get it? Your horses...hold them?

Me: Uhhh...I...

Diversity: Because we are going to travel through time...with a steam engine, instead of a hor—Dude, come on! That was good!

Me: Uhhh, very clever.

Diversity: Thank you, I thought so...anyways, the steam engine didn't, like, revolutionize transportation from walking and wagons to steamships, trains, and automobiles, it completely changed how much work humans can do! But the steam engine didn't just—POOF!—appear overnight...it took a long time.

Me: But, I thought that James Watt invented the steam engine in Scotland in 1776?

Diversity: Woahh...what is up with that year, dude? The Declaration of Independence, *The Wealth of Nations*, annnddd the steam engine?? That's intense...anyway, what were you saying?

Me: Scottish inventor James Watt, steam engines, the Industrial Revolution....

Diversity: Ohhh, yeah, right right. So, this dude, Watt, gets all of the credit, right...like he gets, like, a unit of power named after him, a school named after him, fame, glory, all that good stuff but this other dude, Thomas Newcomen, had already beat him to the punch!

Me: What do you mean "beat him to the punch"? Do you mean James Watt stole the idea from Thomas Newcomen?

Diversity: No, no, it's more like he just aggressively borrowed it and then tweaked it to make the steam engine more awesome…but Thomas Newcomen was already using a version of the steam engine to clear water out of mines. In a weird way, that was even more awesome for James Watt, because you know what powers engines???

Me: People?

Diversity: You're hilarious, dude…coal! It's like a snake eating its tail, dude…like you need coal to power steam engines, but the steam engine was created to mine coal…circle of life man…circle of life.

Me: Diversity…

Diversity: Sorry, dude, what was I saying…oh, yeah, so this steam engine like totally changes EVERYTHING.

Me: Surely you don't mean everything. You know how you can get carried away.

Diversity: Yeah, I do drift but not this time, dude…like really EVERYTHING…check it out. The steam engine didn't just replace animals like horses.

Me: Uhhh…

Diversity: It replaced water and manpower in mines, textile factories, cotton mills, and like a whole bunch of other places.

Me: Okay, though that is impressive it's still not—

Diversity: That's just the beginning, dude! Wrap your noggin around this…almost all the electricity in the world generated from coal or nuclear power is built off of a steam engine, because all engines use some combination of water and heat! Steam engines affect how humans dispose waste or locate drinking water or make clothing! And that's not even the gnarliest part…the steam engine didn't just change what humans could do or make—it changed their lives!

Me: What do you mean, "changed their lives"?

Diversity: Before the Industrial Revolution, like 80 percent of the world were farmers in order to keep themselves and everybody else like…alive. Now, in the United Sates, for example, less than 1 percent of the Americans farm! Before the steam engine, the average life expectancy of a European never rose above 35! And check this out—before the steam engine, it took over a thousand years, from about 200 CE to 1400 CE, for the world population to double from 200 million to 400 million, and by 1650, the world population was about 500 million people. By 1850, the world population doubled to 1 billion! And then, in eight years, the world population doubled again! You know what year is between 1650 and 1850?

Me: 1776??

Diversity: Exxaccctlllyyy…It's not a coincidence that the global birth rate catapults after the invention of Watt's steam engine! But the steam engine didn't just allow people to live long and get their groove on, the steam engine also changed how humans lived…TOGETHER. You remember those horses I told you to hold earlier?

Me: Haha, distinctly.

Diversity: Righteous…so, instead of stables to hold your horses… people created train stations…because there were trains now…because of the steam engine.

Me: Yes, Diversity, I follow.

Diversity: Haha, so, railways facilitated communal transportation but you needed like buildings to maintain this transportation, so they built, like, train stations but you also needed workers to service the people ON the train, so then they hired, like, station masters and ticket sellers and conductors. But then they needed to service passengers when they got OFF the train, so they hired shopkeepers and pharmacists and construction workers. But these professionals had to live near the train stations in order to get to work on time, plus, like I said, these professionals were getting it on with each other and having babies and making families and stuff. So, train hubs needed, like, teachers and doctors, and lawyers and coach drivers, and sanitation workers and policemen and urban administrators to service the families of all the professionals. Eventually, a small urban ecosystem is generated around major train hubs, which attracts even more people because there is a higher chance of earning employment. And, with more people, there are more social classes of people.

Like in eighteenth century England, where the bourgeoise owned the factories, the banks, and the transportation networks and the proletariat worked and maintained the property of the bourgeoise. Then, they had the economic middle class—the doctors, lawyers, and teachers—gluing all of the social classes together. But it didn't just end there! With new social classes of people, you get new ways of organizing these social classes of people, which influences ideas on new societal structures. Like that Marx guy who famously said…"Hey, like, don't work people to death! Their labor is like awesome and way more important than your aristocratic wealth!" And policies like education change from being a total privilege to, like, mandatory. And, soon enough, new ways of thinking create new inventions! Like weapons that can kill multiple people at once, and cars that you don't have to pedal, and beds, and antibiotics, and toilets and contraception and, like, anything humans use to do, like, ANYTHING!

Sooo, yeah, dude, the steam engine changed, like, literally EVERYTHING.

Me: Wow, so I guess you weren't exaggerating.

Diversity: Definitely not, dude, but the point I'm trying to make with the invention of the steam engine is that social progress only happens when humans work dynamically and collaboratively! Thomas Newcomen improved on steam engine designs that came from the Chinese and the Ottomans, and they improved on designs conceived by the Romans! Palm oil was used to grease the textile machines and the palm oil came from the American colonies. And the cotton used to weave fabric came from African slaves. And the textile designs came from Indians. And the coal used to power manufacturing plants came from Britain! If humans just skipped the step where they fight over how different they are and work together, they could create new technologies…technologies that could increase their carrying capacity. Higher carrying capacity, higher chance of survival!

Me: That's actually quite a fascinating theory…but even if humans were able to coordinate effectively to create new technologies, that wouldn't increase the carrying capacity indefinitely. I think our population is close to eight billion and ecologists estimate that the Earth can realistically sustain a human carrying capacity of only about ten to fifteen billion people.

Diversity: Earth has a finite amount of resources but the universe is constantly expanding! Which means, theoretically, the amount of available resources is expanding! Can't humans just, like, try harder to acquire these resources?!!?? To survive!?! Can't they act in their own best interest for, like, one second? The whole world needs them to figure it out! I NEED them to Figure. It. Out!!!

Me: Who are you? Or maybe a better question is, what are you?

Diversity: What??? What are you talking about, dude?

Me: Oh, you don't have to keep up the nineteen seventies "flower power" trope anymore. I can tell that it was just an act.

Diversity: Wow, I knew you were good, but you are really good. What gave it away?

Me: Well, there was definitely some clues early on but what really confirmed my suspicion was when you kept referring to us as "humans" or "people" instead of saying "us" or "we." I mean, once or twice, sure, but every time? It was clear. It was like somehow you were disconnected from people, an outsider looking in…

Diversity: Ooooh…dang, I knew I missed something, haha…gotta remember that for next time.

Me: So, why the spaced-out hippy stereotype anyway? Why not just speak naturally?

Diversity: Was it that bad?

Me: Ehh, I've seen worse.

Diversity: Well, I really did need your help understanding humans. I wanted to seem like a human that would reasonably be concerned with such abstract questions.

Me: And THAT'S what you came up with?

Diversity: Listen! I only materialized twenty minutes before the session. I had to clear your work schedule, find clothes…there was a lot going on. Plus, have you ever created a human brain before? You guys have like a trillion neurons! That's, like, how many stars there are in the galaxy! It takes a while to sort everything out.

Me: Is that why it was so easy for you to mix up names, lose your train of thought, and generally be so "wooaahhh"?

Diversity: Well, in my defense, humans haven't been on the planet as long as animals and plants, so it's kind of hard to remember all of your names individually.

Me: But you knew people like Peter and Rosemary Finch, Robert MacArthur, and Nicolas Laurens Burman perfectly! How are those names easier to remember than Chaka and Genghis Khan?

Diversity: Because, they have something to do with animals, plants, or nature in general! That and the general human stuff is way easier to remember. But give me a break! Like I said, there are a lot of you with a lot of similar names!

Me: Speaking of names…Diversity? Really?

Diversity: Yeah, in the midst of getting everything together, I completely forgot to come up with a name. Ha! I panicked.

Me: Is that why you were always losing your train of thought, as well?

Diversity: Oh, no, that was real. I'm pretty tired and I really haven't slept for, jeesh, I don't know…it's gotta be a couple of hundred thousand years by now.

Me: Wait, how old are you? Wait, before you answer that, you didn't answer my first question…what are you?

Diversity: Well, it's kind of hard to explain but, in short, I'm an atomic force that causes all the variation of our universe…that's kinda why I chose the name Diversity.

Me: I've asked this before, but I'm going to ask this one more time…are you or have you been under the influence recently?

Diversity: Haha, no. I'm serious.

Me: So, how are you here, all at once, in front of me, as a human? Doesn't something need to be protecting the universe right now?

Diversity: It's a big place. It can take care of itself. Are you familiar with the human who came up with the formula $e=mc^2$?

Me: Uhhh, Albert Einstein? Of course, he is one of the most famous physicists of all time!

Diversity: Well, basically, what Albert is eloquently describing is that to create every teensy bit of mass—"M"—you need a whole lot of energy—"E." And I'm talking about a WHOLE LOT…

Me: How much?

Diversity: Well, the C stands for the speed of light in a vacuum and measures about 2.99792458×10^8 m/s…and then square that. That's how much energy you need.

Me: Wow, that is a lot.

Diversity: Yup! So, since humans are made out of cells, which are made out of molecules, which are made out of atoms, which are made out of nuclei, the materialization becomes quite straightforward. You see, the nuclei make up 10^{-15} of the space of an atom but comprise the entire mass of the atom! Did you know that if you took out all of the energy of every human being on the planet, their collective mass would be about the weight of a plum or maybe a peach…if I carry the one—

Me: I did not know that.

Diversity: So, basically, I just borrowed a bunch of energy from some atoms that weren't doing much out there in the universe and mashed up some atoms to be a human so you wouldn't freak out when I talked to you.

Me: Are you GOD? Am I dead right now?

Diversity: Anddd there's the freak-out…this happens every time.

Me: But, how could you be the force that causes all the diversity in the universe? There are…I don't know…gases, fire, bugs, planets! How are you all of that…in one?

Diversity: I am just made out of mass and mass is made out of essentially the same things…quarks, electrons, gluons, bosons…a little bit of—

Me: I still don't understand.

Diversity: Let's take your language, for example. If I arrange the English letters M, A, and D sequentially, I would get the word "MAD," which denotes a certain adverse feeling, correct?

Me: Yes…

Diversity: Ok, but if I added an "E" to the end of this word, I would get a different word with a completely different meaning. Right? The language of the universe is not too different from this. If you add just one more atom to hydrogen—the H in the H2O every human needs to live—you get helium, which, if humans absorbed in large amounts would cause dizziness, headaches, and even suffocation. Sodium is this soft metal that blows up when it reacts to water and chlorine is one of the most reactive and unstable gases that is used to bleach things. If you put them together…you get table salt. Even you—all humans—are just the dust that exploded from stars billions of years ago, which is the same dust that made up planets and galaxies. That's why I fundamentally don't understand why humans keep trying to destroy each other! They are all fundamentally connected…WE are all fundamentally connected!

Me: But, if you are this universal force…why even go to therapy? Don't you know everything?

Diversity: Oh, haha, I'm omnipotent, not omniscient! Man, I wish I knew everything…it would make my life a lot easier. Most of things I create, I do by accident. I kinda just make up things as I go, which is why I came to you! I need your help to sort things out…plus, I feel like nobody is too good for therapy, you know? Great power, great responsibility…man, I love that line. It's sooo true. I'm always stressed out that I'll make a mistake…do you know how many black holes I made accidentally because I blew up a star? Like honestly, it's a lot to manage.

Me: So, why the preoccupation with humans when you have the whole universe to worry about?

Diversity: Because humans have a brain, a mind, and this mind has great power—like imagination. This power, like any power, can lead to creation or it can lead to destruction and I need humans to lean more to the creation side than the destruction side so that they don't destroy other forms of diversity in the universe. Did you know that you guys can create anti-matter in a laboratory?

Me: Why is that a big deal?

Diversity: Do you know what happens to antimatter when it meets matter? Poof! It disappears…the matter turns into pure energy. That's why I can't just ignore the humans or let their little squabbles play out. They could cause annihilations on a catastrophic scale if they don't work together, but it's really hard to figure out how to get them to do that. I need them to work together so their imagination can survive and create more diversity in the universe!

Me: But, why is it so important that humans create more diversity… you ARE Diversity. Haven't you been replicating yourself for billions of years?

Diversity: Yes, but I don't know HOW I do it, I just do it. I don't really know where my power comes from. I don't even know where I come from!

Me: What do you mean?

Diversity: So, I know that when my siblings and I were born—

Me: Siblings!? As in brothers and sisters?

Diversity: Yeah, the other universal forces—gravity, electromagnetism, and the twins, weak and strong nuclear force—which is totally misleading because we are all pretty much the same age, but because strong is a like a little bit older, he thinks he is "stronger" than everybody else…so full of himself, right?

Me: Wow, I have so many thoughts right now.

Diversity: I bet! So, anyway, I was very young, so I don't remember all the details but my siblings told me that when we were born, the universe had about, oh I don't know, $10^{19\text{th}}$ billion electron volts of energy in it. Which means it was very, very hot. Since the universe keeps cooling, there is less energy, so none of us can really say for sure what the universe was like before us. My parents never stuck around long enough to tell us how they got there, or what dimension they are from, or why we have all the power we have.

Me: Is that why you were avoiding talking about your childhood earlier? Because you don't know why you were born?

Diversity: Exactly, that's why I'm fascinated and, frankly, kind of jealous of humans. They don't need to know specifically why something is meaningful. If they don't know why something is important, they can just create importance! But, I can't do that, and if I don't know where my power comes from, I'm afraid that if I lose it one day, I won't be able to get it back. That's why I'm obsessed with and terrified by humans, because they could cause unprecedented amounts of destruction. They can also create unprecedented amounts of meaning and purpose.

Me: Is that why you describe your relationship with your parents as "complicated," because they were never really there to teach you how to use your power?

Diversity: Yeah, it's not like I don't feel them, they are always kind of with me even if they aren't…with me, you know?

Me: I'm not sure I follow.

Diversity: Well, I think you describe them as "Dark Matter" or "Dark Energy," which is weird because though they were kind of absent in my life. I don't think they were "dark" people…you're just not able to detect them because light doesn't travel far away enough to detect them.

Me: So, how could you detect them?

Diversity: Because they cause this gravitational force that's affects me all the time. On all of us...the whole known universe. It's like they are trying to pull me closer to them, but, like, who wants to live with their parents, you know? There is no life out there. There is just...you know... nothingness.

Me: Wow...an existential force having an existential crisis. I think I can retire now. I've seen it all! So, is that why you went to all of this trouble? So you could avoid ending up like your parents? You know, you are not too different from people. Most of us spend our whole lives trying to avoid being like our parents only to end up becoming versions of them anyway. The trick to becoming your own person or, in your case, your own supernatural force, is to learn from your family's mistakes. To embrace the choice to be better, to be more than your past experiences. We might be a flawed and more simplified version of you, but if there's one thing that you can take from humans, it is our optimism. Trust that you are here for a reason, even if you don't know exactly what that reason is, because that's okay! If you don't have a reason, make a reason. Create a purpose. You know, one of my clients recently told me that our lives matter even if, at times, we have to imagine why they matter. The takeaway, I believe, is that if you are any being that has matter, then your existence inherently...well...matters. And maybe that's the best any of us can hope for.

Diversity: I hope so...I need to meditate on that one! I think I'm gonna take a nap...see you later..."dude"

Me: Wait, can you just tell me one more thing...can you just tell me if God is re—

And, it's gone....I could have started my own religion and everything...I guess it's for the best, I suppose...how am I even going to bill for these sessions...

Tape Stops

"Huhh, I still don't know if insurance will accept these notes—guess I'll figure that out in the morning…this has certainly been one strange summer…"

Light switches off.

www.ingramcontent.com/pod-product-compliance
Lightning Source LLC
Chambersburg PA
CBHW020255030426
42336CB00010B/775